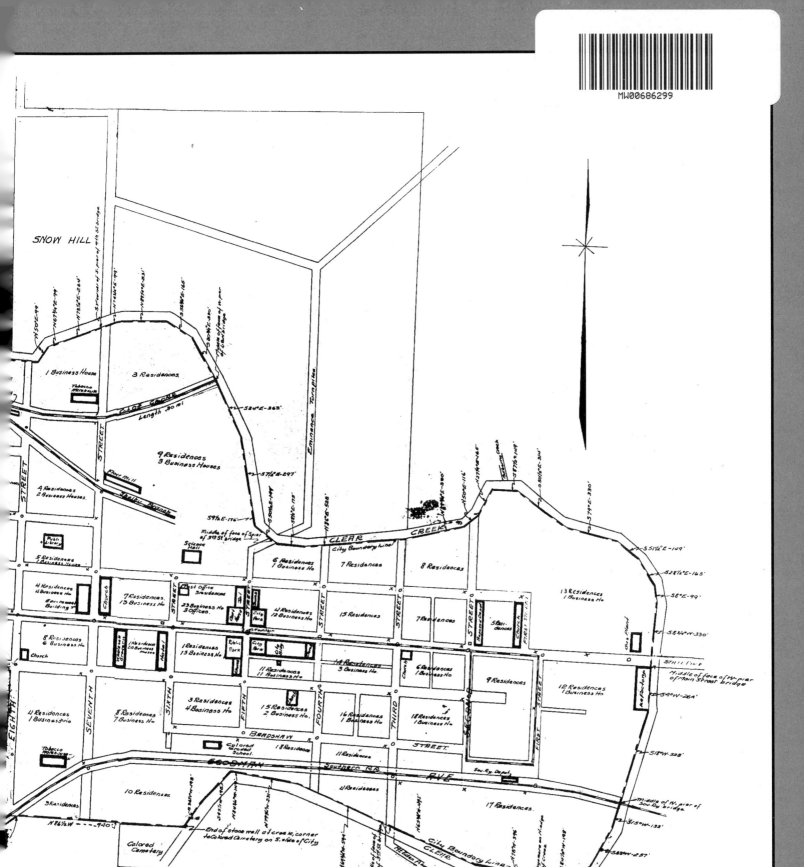

PLAT OF
SHELBYVILLE, KY.
1912
Scale 1" = 250'

GROVE HILL CEMETERY

Portrait of the Past

A Pictorial History of

Shelby County, Kentucky

1865 - 1980

Photos by **Jim Cleveland**   *Text by* **William E. Matthews**

Acclaim Press

Your Next Great Book
P.O. Box 238
Morley, Missouri 63767
(573) 472-9800
www.acclaimpress.com

Library of Congress Control Number: 2008930815
ISBN: 1-935001-05-1
ISBN-13: 978-1-935001-05-8

First Printing 2008
Printed in the United States of America

0 9 8 7 6 5 4 3 2 1

Additional copies may be purchased from Acclaim Press

Cover photo: Stockdale, the federal house on the Eminence Pike, which
was built between 1831 and 1833 for Charles Stewart Todd and his wife
Letitia on land given Letitia in trust by her father, Governor Isaac Shelby.
Charles was the son of U.S. Supreme Court Justice Thomas Todd. Stockdale
is owned by Dr. and Mrs. Lawrence Jelsma who received the Ida Lee Willis
Preservation Project Award from the Kentucky Heritage Council in 1987 for
their renovation of the property.

TABLE OF CONTENTS

FOREWORD

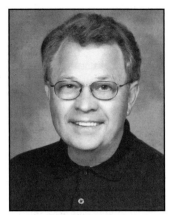

Byron Crawford

Words well-written may touch our hearts and warm our souls, but a photograph has the power to save a moment in time and speak to us beyond words across the years. It is little wonder that family photograph albums are among the most treasured keepsakes in countless homes.

The book you are holding is Shelby County's photographic album and birthright; a remarkable collection of portraits of the county's colorful past from 1865 to 1980. A timeline of historical entries from those 115 years highlights events which were occurring when many of these pictures were made.

Did you know that now famous 20th Century astronomer Edwin Hubble lived briefly in Shelbyville? Or that it was once customary among Democrats for statewide office to open their campaigns at the Shelby County Fairgrounds? Were you aware that two of our presidents, William Howard Taft and Harry S. Truman campaigned here? Were you aware that former Vice-President Alben Barkley, Democrat, and John Sherman Cooper, Republican, were in Shelbyville to promote their candidacies for the U. S. Senate in 1956? Or that 16 inches of snow fell here during one 24-hour period? Did you know that Hall of Fame baseball player and manager Casey Stengel played his first professional game at the old Coots Park in Shelbyville? And did you know that for many years Shelby County was Kentucky's No. 1 agricultural county in terms of gross receipts.

Through the camera lenses of many photographers – most of them professionals, but a few perhaps armed only with a Kodak "Brownie" and a heart for the subject – we are able to view images of both the historic milestones and everyday events during this fascinating era of Shelby County Life.

Among the wealth of subjects remembered in these pages are the businesses and main streets of Shelbyville and surrounding communities, the county's genteel fair and horse show crowds, and its once-numerous tobacco warehouses lined with neat baskets of hand-tied burley, nearly as far as the eye could see. There are glimpses of its movie theaters, its military service personnel, church congregations, early locomotives, pool halls, restaurants, and soda fountains.

A special debt of gratitude is owed to Jim Cleveland and Bill Matthews for their dedicated research and editing of the pictures in this book.

The photographs they chose offer a rich look at where we have been as seen through the eyes of several generations of Shelby County's sons and daughters. The detail and scope of their work certainly assures this book an important place in the county's reference archives. But its most endearing gift to Shelby Countians will be many hours of nostalgic reflection and a greater understanding of our cultural and historic past.

The contributions of those who made this book possible serve to remind us all of the continuing responsibility to photograph and preserve images of our times for those who may hopefully one day add a second and third volume to this work.

Take care to list dates, locations, names and other pertinent biographic information on the back of your photograph to enable an editor in the future to accurately document their importance. Events that may seem unforgettable in the moment soon fade with time. Many images on these pages had long since been obscured by several layers of history and might eventually have become meaningless artifacts without such biographical notes. Instead, they now are the centerpieces of a community keepsake linking Shelby County's yesteryears to its ever-changing present for generations to come.

Place this book within easy reach on the shelf. Its faces, places, and historical footnotes will invite you back again and again.

INTRODUCTION

The most important thing our readers need to know about *Portrait of the Past: A Pictorial History of Shelby County, Kentucky 1865-1980* is that Jim Cleveland deserves most of the credit for this book.

For two, maybe three years Jim, son of Henry and Katherine Cleveland, has been compiling photos, hundreds of photos, from the collections of John Wesley and Otho Williams, Ellis McGinnis, Alwyn and Peggy Miller and his own parents. He has augmented these photos with many others which have been submitted by hundreds of Shelby County citizens anxious to have the county's wonderful heritage preserved.

It would be difficult to calculate the thousands of hours which Jim has put into the project, and he has done it with great enthusiasm, much curiosity, a willingness to research the particulars of each photo, and has been careful with the facts.

This book starts with images from the Civil War or the War Between the States and ends with Martha Layne Collins election as Lieutenant Governor and Shelby County's state championship baseball team. In between there are photos of schools, politicians, basketball teams, fires, everyday citizens, blue ribbon cattle, train trips and wrecks, kindergarten classes, Latin banquets, a Hall of Fame football player, and many family gatherings. There are four different presidents (Jimmy Carter, Gerald Ford, William Howard Taft, and Harry Truman) meeting or talking with Shelby Countians, and a former vice-president, Alben Barkley, making his final appearance in Shelby County as a Democratic candidate for the U.S. Senate he had held many years ago. His opponent, John Sherman Cooper, is also here competing for the same seat in the U. S. Congress. Three Kentucky Governors, Bert Combs, A. B. Chandler, and Wendell Ford grace these pages, all of this pointing out how important Shelby County has been to those on the national and state scene.

A timeline from 1865 to 1980 gives one to three pertinent facts about each of those 115 years. You will learn in what year the lights were turned on in downtown Shelbyville, the year that the mayor ordered all adults to be vaccinated against smallpox, the year that the People's Deposit Bank of Shelbyville was forced to close because of a longtime embezzlement, and learn again about all of the personalities involved in the trial and cold-blooded murder of Gen. H. H. Denhardt.

This timeline tells about the rationing of food and tires in World War II, and the death of the first Shelby County soldier, Arvil Yeary, in that conflict. Several of Coach Evan Settle's state tournament teams are featured as are, naturally, the 1966 and 1978 Shelby County Rockets basketball teams. You will read about Shelby County's outstanding success as a tobacco market and agricultural leader, and about the men and women who contributed to that success.

This book contains images of several thousand Shelby Countians and their homes and ways of life. It gives varying insights as to how they dressed, what cars they drove, and how well their families and communities fared.

Jim Cleveland and I have enjoyed bringing these pages together. It is a rather modest, yet we believe comprehensive, contribution to our county's history. We hope you will take pleasure from our research and appreciate anew what a remarkably grand and historic county we live in.

William E. Matthews

William E. Matthews

Panoramic view from Clay Street of the 1909 fire that destroyed much of the south side of the 500 block of Main Street.

HISTORIC IMAGES

FROM COURT HOUSE LOOK'TO KNOBS. 1876
WILLIAMS

TIME LINE FOR SHELBY COUNTY, KENTUCKY
1865 TO 1980

1865 The Civil War or The War Between the States ends in April. The following month the Shelby Home Guard under Edwin Terrell hunts down and mortally wounds infamous guerrilla William Quantrill near Wakefield in Spencer County. Quantrill and another infamous guerrilla, "Sue Mundy" had been involved in the massacre of 22 colored soldiers in January, 1865 near Simpsonville. John William Shannon begins a funeral tradition in Oldham County which will continue to the present day in Shelby County.

1866 Democrat John Stevenson is elected governor.

1867 Democrat John L. Helms wins over Republican Sidney M. Barnes and Union Democrat William B. Kincaid.

1868 David Todd Stuart, founder of Stuart's College, dies. The U. S. Senate, sitting as a court of impeachment, fails by one vote to convict President Andrew Johnson of the charges levied against him.

1869 Bank of Shelbyville starts operations. Scholars observe eclipse of the sun from the observatory atop Shelby College on College Street.

1870 A. Rothchild Co. clothing company is established on 6th Street in Shelbyville (it would survive for more than 80 years). Alice Hegan Rice, who was to find national fame as an author with her "Mrs. Wiggs of the Cabbage Patch," is born in Shelbyville. Shelby County is state's No. 1 agricultural county. Democrat Preston O. Leslie is elected governor. Shelby County census is 15,733.

1871 The Ku Klux Klan (KKK) is organized at Bagdad. Shelby Railroad Company begins operation between Shelbyville and Anchorage. Floral Hall is built at the Fairgrounds. Farmers & Traders Bank is incorporated, with J. D. Guthrie as president.

1872 The Louisville, Cincinnati, and Lexington Railroad Company purchases for $23,000 per mile the branch railroad from Anchorage to Shelbyville. In eastern Shelby County masked men burn down the barn of negro Lawson Johnson and kill Gabe Flood, but are driven off. Elizabeth Cady Stanton lectures in Louisville in favor of woman's suffrage. A minister there calls her the leader of an "infidel assault upon our social order and civilization."

1873 KKK band attacks houses of several negroes in Beatty's Mill, five miles from Simpsonville. At Clay Village men stone a black family and kill a white man who comes to their assistance. Great financial "panic" begins a major depression in businesses in Shelby County and across the country. The Kentucky legislature passes an act providing two dollars for each wolf scalp, and one dollar for fox and wildcat scalps to reduce the number of wild animals roaming the countryside.

1874 Democrat James B. McCreary is elected governor.

1875 Two schools for colored students are now operating. Simpsonville Christian Church is dedicated.

1876 First post office is established at Finchville with Samuel O. Mitchell as postmaster. Methodist church is organized at Finchville.

1877 Kentuckian John Marshall Harlan is named to the U.S. Supreme Court; later he will be acknowledged as one of the nation's greatest justices.

1878 Joseph P. Foree is elected Shelby County Judge. Democrat Luke Blackburn is elected governor. Henri F. Middleton, first secretary of Grove Hill Cemetery, dies.

1879 Woman's Missionary Circle is organized at Simpsonville.

1880 The Louisville, Cincinnati and Lexington Railroad Company establishes a line, which runs from Shelbyville through Finchville to Bloomfield. Census is 16,603 for Shelby County.

1881 John Vonderheide, a white man charged with raping and murdering a white girl, is the last person legally executed in Shelby County.

1882 L. G. "Pop" Smith enters pharmacy business (co-founder of Smith-McKenney). The KKK attacks Stringtown, a community of freed slaves between Bagdad and Hatton. Several negroes are killed and their homes burned.

The blockhouse erected in the late 1850s served to protect the citizens of Shelbyville against attack, and was positioned near the courthouse where arms were stored. The photograph is from 1865.

Left: Edwin Terrell, who fought for both the North and South during the Civil War, later headed up the Shelby Home Guard which on May 10, 1865 trapped famed Confederate guerrilla William Quantrill and his raiders near Wakefield in Spencer County. Quantrill was mortally wounded in the ensuing battle. In May, 1866 Terrell, who was to be tried for murdering a traveling salesman, was gunned down as he emerged from the Armstrong Hotel at the corner of 6th and Main Streets. He was 26 years of age when he died.

William Clarke Quantrill, the most infamous of all the Civil War guerrillas and remembered for the "Massacre of Lawrence, Kansas" in August, 1863, was a participant in the massacre of black soldiers near Simpsonville in January 1865. He was only 27 years of age when he died in a military prison in Louisville on June 6, just 27 days after he had been wounded.

Jerome Marcellus Clarke, alias "Sue Mundy", was with Quantrill when the guerrillas massacred 22 black soldiers herding a cattle train to Louisville in January, 1865. He was executed on March 15, 1865, on orders of General Palmer, military commander of Kentucky, after he and several colleagues were captured in Meade County. He was 20 years old when his life was ended at the end of a rope. A historical marker at 10th & Broadway in Louisville marks his execution.

Members of the Harvard Astronomical expedition came to Shelby College (on the site of the old Northside School and Old Graded School) to observe the solar eclipse of August 7, 1869. Some of the local townsfolk who can be identified by their numbers include 1. Dr. Otho Miller. 2. Capt. W. C. Winlock. 3. Miss Eliza Winlock. 4. Mrs. Belle Winlock (of Cambridge, Massachusetts), 5. Dr. R. F. Logan, 6. Miss Anna Powell. 7. Capt. Marion Taylor (who served with the Union during the Civil War), 8. Frank Adams, St. Louis, MO., 9. John Tate. 10. Honorable James S. Morris, 11. R. C. Tevis. 12. Prof. Joseph Winlock (Cambridge), 13. Ed. D. Shinnick. 14. George A. Armstrong 15. Prof. Ray Pierce (Cambridge), 16. Samuel Wayne. and 17. The servant and cook in the family of Judge Fielding Winlock of Shelbyville. The four children seated on the ground between No. 3 and No. 7 and the rear of No. 9 are the children of Prof. Joseph Winlock of Cambridge. 18. Daniel Baker. All of the individuals in the photo are from Shelbyville unless otherwise identified.

1883 Southern Railway begins service to Shelby County. Adam Middleton is elected president of Shelby County Agricultural & Mechanical Fair.

1884 Shelbyville Water and Light Company provides first electric light service to the city streets in December. Bagdad Roller Mills begins as a manufacturer of flour. Morse School of Telegraphy opens. First Masonic Hall is built on Washington Street between 5th and 6th Streets.

1885 Olive Branch United Methodist Church membership is largest in Shelby County.

1886 First public school opens in Finchville. Shelby Academy operated by Thomas and Rowena Doolan closes. Former Confederate General Simon Bolivar Buckner is elected governor. *The Shelby News* is founded by John P. Cozine.

1887 The Shelby County Trust Bank (now Commonwealth Bank & Trust) was incorporated, with J. A. Weakley as president.

1888 Waddy is established, named after former Confederate Major W. L. Waddy who donated the land for the railroad depot. The Citizens Bank (now Citizens Union) was incorporated with Charles Kinkel as its first president. Peoples Bank of Bagdad, the first bank institution chartered in Shelby County outside the city of Shelbyville, opens.

1889 Bagdad Baptist Church is founded. James P. Vannatta is the new Shelbyville postmaster.

1890 Cropper is incorporated. Democrat John Young Brown is elected governor. Shelby County census is 16,601.

1891 American Saddlebred Horse Association registers first horse farm in Shelby County. Glacier Ice Company begins operating. W. H. Tipton is elected county judge.

1892 New stone jail built at the corner of 5th and Washington Streets in Shelbyville. Thomas Baxter begins 18 years of service on the Shelbyville City Council (Baxter is the first black man elected to a city council position in Kentucky).

1893 Chapel dedicated at Grove Hill Cemetery, Lewis Henry Gruber and Sons having been commissioned to build the structure. Several from Shelby County attend the second inauguration of President Grover Cleveland. New Presbyterian Church is dedicated at the corner of 7th & Washington Streets. "Money panic" nationally has few repercussions in Shelby County.

1894 John I. Logan is elected mayor of Shelbyville. The "Enterprise" newspaper is started in Waddy. Waddy Roller Mills and Waddy Normal School "going strong." Republican William O. Bradley is elected governor.

1895 Shelbyville gets a public water system, eliminating the need for cisterns which were believed to be the cause of several outbreaks of cholera. Telephone service comes to Shelbyville. The rail line is extended to Christiansburg. Shelby Hop Club gives its annual Christmas Day dance at Layson's Opera House at the corner of 7th and Main Streets.

1896 Salem Baptist Church re-dedicated after a disastrous fire. St. Johns Methodist Church is built on College Street in Shelbyville.

1897 Centenary United Methodist Church is dedicated.

1898 Luther Willis begins eight-year term as mayor. New post office established at Joyes Station. Mass meeting calls for removal of tolls on turnpike. The Kings Daughters Hospital is chartered.

1899 Shelby County Chapter of the Daughters of the American Revolution organized; Anna McClarty Harbison is first Regent. Shelby County had 48 white and 19 colored schools.

1900 Electric lights are turned on in downtown Shelbyville. John Logan elected president of Shelbyville Water and Light Company. Three Shelby County men who had served in the Confederate "Orphan Brigade" attend the annual reunion. Mt. Eden bank opens. Census for Shelby County is 18,340.

1901 Old Masons Home is established in Shelbyville.

1902 First Kentucky State Fair is held at Churchill Downs. Confederate Home is established at Pewee Valley for care of aging, infirm veterans of the Civil War.

1903 Carnegie Library opens. United Confederate Veterans elect Dr. William F. Beard, Commander, Virgil Lewis, Lt. Commander, and R. T. Owen, Adjutant. George Chowning elected president of the Shelbyville Commercial Club. First hospital opens on Clay Street.

1904 Bank of Finchville opens with J. W. Hardin president and W. C. Winlock cashier (it merged with the Bank of Shelbyville in 1931).

1905 Shelbyville native Dan McGann captained the New York Giants in the World Series. Cropper Bank opens.

The total solar eclipse of August 7, 1869.

This is how 5th and Main Streets, facing north, in Shelbyville appeared in 1874.

Shelbyville can be seen in the distance in this photo taken from Grove Hill Cemetery in 1876.

Elijah Marrs, slave, Union soldier, educator, Baptist minister, Republican politician, and an early advocate of African-American civil rights, was born in January, 1840 in Shelby County. On September 26, 1864, Marrs, with 26 other Shelby County slaves, enlisted in the Union army, having led them from Simpsonville to the recruiting office in Louisville. Marrs opened a school in Simpsonville in 1866 and taught more than 100 students that first year. On August 3, 1871, Marrs married Julia Gray, daughter of Harriet Gray of Shelby County. They lived on Main Street in Shelbyville in a two-story frame house that Marrs had built prior to the wedding. She died in 1876 and is buried in the Shelbyville cemetery. Elijah Marrs lived until August 30, 1910. He is buried in Louisville's Greenwood Cemetery.

1906 Post office at Southville discontinued. Bank of Waddy fails (warrant issued for arrest of bank president T. B. Hancock). Shelby County native Brigadier Gen. J. Franklin Bell heads up the U. S. Army. Kings Daughters Hospital opens on Clay Street.

1907 Charles Marshall begins 36 years of service as circuit judge. Carrie Nation appears at Layson Hall and First Christian Church and lectures on the evils of strong drink.

1908 City Council orders every adult citizen to be vaccinated against smallpox. Shelby County native Dan McGann leads National League in fielding, fifth in batting average. William Howard Taft campaigns in Shelbyville on behalf of his presidential candidacy.

1909 Bonds issued to build new courthouse. Lynn Gruber elected mayor of Shelbyville. Fire destroys several Main Street buildings, including the First Baptist Church. An outbreak of smallpox reaches epidemic proportions, causing school to be suspended for several weeks.

1910 Future Hall of Famer Casey Stengel plays baseball for Maysville against Shelbyville in a Bluegrass League game at Coots Park, just off 2nd Street. Free mail delivery begins. Beautiful new onyx soda fountain installed at Smith-McKenney. Interurban begins service between Louisville and Shelbyville. Future Rhodes Scholar, astronomer Edwin Hubble lives briefly with family at 928 Bland Avenue in Shelbyville. Shelby County census is 18,004.

1911 W. P. Deiss establishes his bookstore on Main Street between 5th & 6th Streets. Mob lynches two black men, Gene Marshall and Wade Patterson. Lincoln Institute opens near Simpsonville, aided by a $200,000 bequest from Andrew Carnegie. The new First Baptist Church is dedicated.

1912 Leon Rothchild begins 10-year stint as Shelbyville mayor. Bagdad builds it first high school on land donated by George Sacra. Simpsonville High School dedicated. Shelbyville Chautauqua Club is organized with 16 members.

1913 Todd's Point post office closes. The Kentucky Utilities is awarded a franchise to provide light and power to Shelby County for 20 years. Local businessman Charles Schradski places a five light, 100 candlepower lamp post in front of his business on Washington Street.

1914 The new Shelby County courthouse opens for business. Allen Dale farm's Raleigh, owned by Sue Henning, is judged the national grand champion Jersey bull at the National Dairy Show. Lawson's Department Store opens.

1915 Shelby County native A. O. Stanley elected governor of Kentucky. Bohn's Creamery (which became famous for its ice creams made with fresh fruit) opens for business at 2nd & Washington Streets. Drs. W. T. Buckner and A. C. Weakley form partnership for the practice of medicine.

1916 Gleneyrie High School is dedicated.

1917 42 Shelby County men are called to duty as nation enters World War I. Admission price raised to 20 cents at local music hall. Students begin attending the new Shelbyville High School.

1918 Worst blizzard in recorded county history deposits 16 inches of snow in 24 hours, the temperature dips to 16 degrees below zero. World War I's end finds many Shelby County men on their way home from foreign lands. Hempridge Baptist Church is dedicated.

1919 Flu epidemic kills thousands of Kentuckians, death toll includes many Shelby Countians. George Wells, Confederate veteran and former sheriff, dies at Veechdale.

1920 New motion picture show opens between 6th & 7th on Main Street. Sheriff collects $319,066.65 in county and state taxes. Paul Schmidt begins the production of Coca-Cola on Henry Clay Street in Shelbyville.

1921 The only bank ever to exist in Cropper fails. Todd's Point school opens. New Louisville-Lexington bus service offered by Harold O. and James Barnes begins operation with two seven-passenger Studebaker automobiles.

1922 Curtis Hall elected mayor by the City Council. New brick school built at Waddy, combining schools at Lone Oak and Elm Hill. E. J. Paxton is the principal.

1923 Leo and Alberta Riester begin operating a store in Finchville. Building & Loan Association is organized with Herbert Maddox president, Moses Ruben vice-president. County officials H. B. Kinsolving Jr. and Deputy Sheriff John Dawson Buckner confiscate 30 gallons of moonshine and 600 gallons of mash.

1924 The J. Franklin Bell American Legion Post is established in Shelbyville. Mt. Eden High School graduates its first class. Otis Wright appointed Shelbyville Police Chief. New Ford from Detroit costs $295 FOB Detroit. Shelbyville Church of Christ moves into its new building on Washington Street.

The railroad came to Shelby County in the 1870s.

Shelbyville's South Main Street at 5th Street was a developing town in 1882.

Local citizens in 1876 had this view of Main Street east looking toward the Knobs.

1925 Thieves break into Shelbyville post office and carry off all of the local mail. W. H. Tipton is re-elected president of Citizens Bank. Native Shelby Countian J. Franklin Bell awarded Distinguished Service Cross posthumously by U. S. Army. Lindsey Logan and Jeptha Bright purchase Shelbyville steam laundry and building.

1926 George L. Willis Jr. is elected county judge. Rev. Charles Elsey assumes pastorate of Shelbyville's First Baptist Church.

1927 Otho H. Vardaman is sentenced to 16 years in the state penitentiary for embezzling more than $61,000 from the Deposit Bank of Shelbyville. The bank closed the same day the embezzlement was discovered. The money was never recovered. The Shelbyville Rotary Club is chartered by the Frankfort Rotary Club; B. B. Cozine is the first president. Barney Bright, who was to enjoy national fame as a sculptor, is born in Shelbyville. The Biagi Company starts doing business as a tire company.

1928 Work begins on rebuilding the Elks Home on Washington Street.

1929 George L. Willis Sr. publishes *The History of Shelby County*. Stock market crash in October has people wondering about jobs and the economy.

1930 World War I mothers of those killed in action are invited to visit their sons' graves at government expense. Paul F. Schmidt is elected Shelbyville mayor by the City Council.

1931 George and Daisy Mildred Saffell start a funeral home at 4th and Clay Streets.

1932 Services on the Interurban end after 22 years. Four men rob the Bank of Simpsonville. The Shelby County Chamber of Commerce is incorporated with Paul F. Schmidt president.

1933 Shelby County votes overwhelmingly to repeal 18th amendment (prohibition of alcohol). City Council votes to build municipal electric plant. First machinery arrives at the Lee-McClain & Scalzo plant (Lee-McClain would become a preeminent clothing manufacturer until its demise in the 1990s). An office is opened to serve all of the "unemployed." Schools abolished include Pea Ridge, Cat Ridge, Locust Grove, Camden, Maple Hall, Fox Run and Elmburg. Bus fare from Shelbyville to Louisville is reduced to 70 cents.

1934 Repaved U. S. 60 between Shelbyville and Middletown opens. New theatre, The Shelby opens (formerly the Bon-Ton). Robert. F. Matthews begins what will turn out to be nearly 20 years service as Shelbyville mayor. Famed Cross Keys Inn on U. S. 60 near Graefenburg is destroyed by fire. The Marquis deLafayette, on his famous triumphant return to the United States, had stayed there in 1825.

1935 Gleneyrie opens its new gymnasium. Tobacco sells for $9.94 per 100 lbs. Civilian Conservation Camp (CCC) planned.

1936 Future Governor Martha Layne Collins (nee Hall) is born at the King's Daughters Hospital in Shelbyville, the daughter of Mary and Everett Hall of Bagdad. Shelby County goes strongly for Roosevelt for a second term. Shelbyville ties Lexington Henry Clay, 6-6, wins CKC football title. Gen. H. H. Denhardt is charged with the murder of Verna Garr Taylor. Portia Book Club begins with 10 members.

1937 Roy and Jack Garr are acquitted in slaying of Gen. H. H. Denhardt. "Great Flood" finds thousands of refugees being provided for in Shelbyville churches and school gym. New Coca-Cola plant welcomes local residents at open house.

1938 City Council votes $40,000 for model sewage treatment plant. New road between Finchville and Mt. Eden approved. Paul Schmidt donates 300 dogwood trees to the city. A new bus station opens between 6th and 7th Streets on Main Street. Low tobacco prices have farmers seeking crop controls and quotas.

1939 Shelby farmers relieved as U. S. Supreme Court rules tobacco quotas constitutional. Prominent lawyer and U. S. Congressman Ralph Gilbert dies suddenly while campaigning for lieutenant governor. Jackie Byrd wins first of three straight high school tennis titles. Science Hill School closes after 114 years of continuous operation.

1940 George Giles is named county school superintendent. Nine county schools graduate 141 young men and women. Five men named to Shelby Draft Board as war looms. A new airport is being planned for the county.

1941 Louis C. Wingfield is the first name called as 40 are summoned for the draft. Record crowd attends tobacco festival, watches Jack Green star as locals upset Lexington Henry Clay, 14-7 in football. Roger Palmer is aboard the U.S.S. Oklahoma when the Japanese attack Pearl Harbor. 40 new buses begin service between Louisville and Lexington via Shelbyville.

1942 Tire and sugar rationing begin. Alex Veech, Finchville, is named "Kentucky Farmer of the Year." Shelbyville Tobacco Board of Trade is organized.

In the late 1890s this panoramic view shows Main Street and 6th Street adjoined.

The Shelby County Agricultural and Mechanical Fair was held on these grounds and in these buildings in the 1880s. Note the cupola atop the Floral Hall building.

In 1892 the Gruber family, famous for many of the buildings that still grace Shelby County, gathered at their home on East Main Street. At the left is Lynn Thomas Gruber, his wife Mamye Deets, with daughters Bertie and Grace (seated in front); at right is Henry Calvin Gruber, wife Mettie Davis and children John Lewis and Helen Kate. Seated in the center are Lucy Catherine Dear and Lewis Henry Gruber.

In the 1890s Main Street offered this view facing east from 5th Street.

1943 Interurban rails removed for scrap for war effort. $200,000 in war bonds sold locally. Arvil Yeary, Christiansburg, becomes the first Shelby County man killed in action in World War II. Sgt. Allen Phillips is killed in France. Dempsie Poe named chairman of the ration board. Shortage of teachers due to war causes school board to hire two ministers to teach.

1944 German war prisoners are working on 175 Shelby County farms.

1945 Shelby County's Jack Green captains West Point's national championship football team (he was later elected to the National Football Hall of Fame). Fred Trammel begins a farming class for returning veterans.

1946 L. G. "Pop" Smith, "Shelby County's most beloved citizen" dies. City Council votes to build municipal swimming pool. Memorial services honor the 57 men from Shelby County who died in action, accidents, or disease in World War II. Shelbyville Kiwanis Club is chartered.

1947 The Maddox-Yeary VFW Club is organized in Shelbyville, honoring Arvil Yeary, first World War II casualty from the county, and "Monk" Maddox from the city. Shelby Flying Service organized on land owned by Clarence Catlett Sr. Finchville Farms Country Hams begins operations under Bill Robertson.

1948 Harry F. Walters is named State Commissioner of Agriculture. County school board plans new central high school. Shelbyville High School goes to state basketball tournament for first time, beats Garrett, loses to eventual state champion Brewers. Dr. Maurice Rabb, who would go on to practice medicine for 50 years in Shelbyville and Louisville, becomes the first African-American to train at Louisville's General Hospital.

1949 Roll Forming begins operations on Goodman Ave. & 1st Street. State school board threatens to de-certify six county schools, including Waddy, Mt. Eden, Finchville, Henry Clay, Cropper and Gleneyrie because of low student enrollment. Bruce Sweeney is elected president of the new Lions Club in Simpsonville. City Council approves extending Washington Street and making it one way west, Main Street to become one way east. Finchville graduates its final high school class.

1950 Judge Roy Bean is alleged to have been born near Simpsonville. City pays off parking meters, calls for tougher enforcement to improve parking. Shelby County named state's No. 1 farm county, with total revenues of over $20 million. The city swimming pool opens for whites only. Pfc. Edward Julian Wilson became Shelby County's first casualty of the Korean War (eight Shelby Countians became fatal victims of the conflict).

1951 First class stamp goes to 4 cents. Septic tanks, drainage systems and indoor toilets replace outdoor toilets at six county high schools. Five eastern Shelby County communities organize combined rural fire department. Fire destroys Burks Branch Baptist Church.

1952 Bagdad High School wins 8th region basketball title, advances to Kentucky High School tournament where it loses in the opening round.

1953 First Ruritan Club is organized at Bagdad, with Wesley Newton president. Shelbyville upsets Owensboro in state basketball tournament, loses to Paducah in quarter-finals. Joe Bowles named to All-Tournament team. New Burks Branch Baptist Church dedicated.

1954 Willie Fleming, valedictorian at Lincoln Institute, is among the first two black graduates of the University of Louisville Law School. Harold Saunders defeats William Chenault to succeed Robert Matthews as Shelbyville mayor. New county hospital is dedicated. "Timely Tip," owned by Dr. A. L. Birch, finishes 14th in the Kentucky Derby. Shelbyville is visited by a Southern Railroad passenger train for the last time.

1955 Purnell sausage plant opens in Simpsonville.

1956 Shelby County voters join rest of nation in supporting Dwight Eisenhower's re-election.

1957 Shelby County Industrial and Development Foundation is organized. Charles and Helen Crabtree and son Redd launch Crabtree Farms near Simpsonville.

1958 Jesse Puckett begins the first of three terms as mayor of Shelbyville. Shelbyville loses to Bowling Green in opening round of state basketball tournament. Ceiling of First Baptist Church collapses.

1959 Contract let to build a new municipal building at the corner of 11th and Main. New Shelby Lake named for Governor A. B. Chandler (it would later be renamed Guist Creek Lake during the Bert Combs administration).

1960 Col. and Mrs. Harland D. Sanders establish their residence on U. S. 60, five miles from Shelbyville. Bruce Sweeney is named principal of the new consolidated Shelby County High School. Fires badly damage Lincoln Institute and Scofield Pharmacy. Mrs. W. C. Ray retires after 30 years as city school superintendent. John F. Kennedy edges Richard Nixon for U. S. President.

Shelby County's premier mercantile family, the Rothchilds, gathered in 1898. Standing, from left to right, are May, Bettie, Edwin, and Helene; seated, from left, Leon, Sallie, Henry, Abraham, and Clementine.

The storefront of George Petry's business at the corner of 6th and Main is clearly visible in 1890.

Main Street was busy with horse-and-buggies and many pedestrians in 1896.

A mass baptism in Brashears Creek drew quite a crowd of onlookers at the turn of the 20th century.

1961 Wakefield-Scearce Galleries is established by Mark J. Scearce. New water plant planned at Guist Creek Lake.

1962 Moses Ruben dies, and leaves his entire estate to King's Daughters Hospital (now the Shelby County Community Foundation).

1963 The Shelbyville municipal swimming pool is integrated without incident. Mrs. Purcell Lee is elected first president of the Shelby County Historical Society. Mary Louise Foust, who served three terms as state auditor, loses her bid to become Kentucky's first woman governor. Robert F. Matthews Jr. becomes the first Shelby Countian elected Attorney General of Kentucky. Asian flu hits estimated 1,000 Shelby Countians.

1964 I-64 opens between Shelbyville and Louisville. Col. Harland D. Sanders sells Kentucky Fried Chicken for $2 million to group headed by John Y. Brown Jr. School Superintendent Bill McKay elected president of Kentucky Association of Fairs and Horse Shows. Jake Brummett replaces Roy S. Jones as the city's new police chief.

1965 Bagdad dedicates its new post office. KFC elects John Y. Brown Jr. president. Roscoe Poe kills two men who try to burglarize his home near Finchville. Sam Hinkle, a senior at Shelbyville High School, is named a National Merit Scholarship finalist. No. 1 rated Shelby County Rockets (30-1) lose to eventual state champion Breckinridge County in the quarter-finals after beating Clark County in the opening game of the state basketball tournament.

1966 Paul J. McGaughey of Southville becomes the first Shelby County casualty of the Vietnam conflict. Shelby County Rockets beat Male High School, 52-47, to win the Kentucky State Basketball title. Mike Casey is named Kentucky's "Mr. Basketball." Lincoln Institute graduates its last class. A kindergarten operated by Mrs. Mary David Myles starts operating (it closed in 1987). New junior high school approved east of Shelbyville at a cost of $600,000.

1967 Lee Nor Mack, an African-American, begins what will eventually become an 18-year stint as Shelbyville City councilman (only one other African-American had ever served on the Council). Shelbyville High School wins 8th region title, loses to Monticello in its opening game of Kentucky State High School Basketball Tournament.

1968 Terry Davis is named Kentucky's "Mr. Basketball," averaging 35.5 points a game at Shelby County High. Rev. Kenneth Shouse is called to lead the new Shelby Christian Church. St. James Episcopal Church observes its 100th anniversary. New highway marker honors Bland W. Ballard, survivor of Tick Creek massacre, and legendary pioneer. Highland Baptist Church holds its first services. Shelby County loses to Caneyville in the quarter-finals of state basketball tournament. Mrs. Clarence Miller succeeds Mrs. Betsy Schmidt as local Republican chairman. Willie Fleming speaks out for more economic opportunities for blacks in Shelby County. Coleman Wright voted Kentucky's Most Outstanding Judge.

1969 Roll Forming employees reject unionization. Elmo Head named president of Farmers & Traders Bank. Shelbyville's First Christian Church burns. New First Baptist Church is dedicated.

1970 Memorial services honor the 14 men killed in the Vietnam conflict. Wyman Porter begins four-term as mayor (he accepted no pay while in office). Talk of a possible jetport causes concern in western end of the county.

1971 Ed "Hoppy" Bennett enters the saddlebred horse business at Bennett Farms on Taylorsville Road. The C & O's George Washington makes its final stop in Shelbyville, ending rail service after 101 years.

1972 *The Shelby Sentinel* and *The Shelby News* merge to form *The Sentinel-News*.

1973 Sammy Wood is elected sheriff. Finchville chosen as site for a new jetport. Landmark Communications buys Newspapers Inc., names William E. Matthews president. Don Chatham praised for saving L&N railroad station. The home where President Harry Truman's grandparents were married at Christiansburg is remodeled.

1974 Marshall Long begins the first of two terms as Shelbyville mayor. Marvin Rogers is the new Shelbyville postmaster. First meeting of the newly merged city and county school boards. Fred Bond succeeds Ralph Mitchell as county judge. Mitchell forms law partnership with Harold Saunders.

1975 The Shelby County Woman's Club is organized with Pam Evans as its first president.

1976 Sam Chandler is new Shelby County High School principal. Howard Logan Jr. wins state high school golf title.

1977 The Shelby County Community Theatre offers its first production, "The Music Man" under the direction of Robert Shy. Republic Bank begins operating in Shelby County following its acquisition of the People's Bank of Bagdad. Clear Creek Park dedicated, Dr. Ron Waldridge

This was one of several covered bridges that once served Shelby County. This one overlooked Benson Creek near Graefenburg.

Another covered bridge protected those who crossed Clear Creek on Jail Hill road.

This covered bridge crossed Clear Creek on East Main Street.

considered the park's father. New Mt. Zion Baptist Church moves from Waddy to the Washington Street building once used by the Church of Christ.

1978 Shelby County Rockets defeat Covington Holmes, 68-66 to win their second state basketball championship. Mike George, Norris Beckley, and Charles Hurt were named to the All-Tournament team. The Methodist Centenary Church is destroyed by fire. Tom Easterly upsets John Breckinridge in congressional race. First class stamp jumps from 13 to 15 cents. Sue Carole Perry is elected county clerk. New elementary school to be built east of Shelbyville.

1979 Shelby County Rockets win state high school baseball title, with Tracy Driver voted Most Valuable Player. Patrons enjoy the new addition at the library. Water service comes to Finchville. Martha Layne Collins wins election as lieutenant-governor.

1980 The new post office opens at 4th and Main Streets. New Production Credit Association building is dedicated. Shelby County census puts county population at 22,783. Ronald Reagan is elected president, but Democrat Jimmy Carter carries Shelby County.

Built in 1791, the Benjamin Washburn home on Bellevue Road near Cropper served as the home place for three generations of Washburns. The house, which stood in three counties (Shelby, Jefferson, and Fincastle), was built in simple, unadorned, Colonial style. It deteriorated to the point that it had to be demolished in the late 1960s.

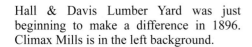

Hall & Davis Lumber Yard was just beginning to make a difference in 1896. Climax Mills is in the left background.

Fire destroyed several buildings in the 500 block on the south side of Main Street on Feb. 11, 1899.

Sidney Ramey Hundley, grandfather of Lamar Hundley Jr., shoeing a horse circa, 1900.

This early 1900s photo shows the corner of 6th and Main Streets. Note the primitive streetlight, five-deck telephone poles, and the cupola atop the courthouse.

Shelby County native Alice Hegan Rice became Shelby County's most famous author with the publication of "Mrs. Wiggs of the Cabbage Patch" in 1901.

A cakewalk competition at the Shelby County Fairgrounds was sponsored by the African-American community in the early 1900s.

The historic Armstrong Hotel was located at the southwest corner of 6th and Main Streets. Many years later it would serve as the backdrop for the killing of Brig. Gen. Henry H. Denhardt by the three Garr brothers who blamed Gen. Denhardt for the alleged murder of their sister, Verna Garr Taylor.

A crowd of citizens with their horse-and-buggies gathered at the intersection of 5th and Main Streets in 1904. The fountain was then in the middle of the intersection. Several years later it was moved to the adjacent courtyard to make room for the Interurban tracks.

Motor cars were traveling on Main Street between 4th and 5th Streets in the early 1900s.

William Howard Taft came to Shelbyville in 1909 on behalf of his candidacy for the U. S. Presidency.

This Mt. Eden band was ready to entertain all those who would listen in 1910. In the front are Forest Snider, Edgar Waters, and Bill Cleveland; back, Jim Hedden, Henry G. Cleveland, Ott Snider, and Ottis Goodwin.

Farmers were busy delivering their tobacco to the Continental Tobacco Warehouse in the early 1900's.

Pius Roemmele was a substantial landowner and farmer who in 1910 was known for his deliveries of tobacco, potatoes, turnips, and strawberries.

Shelby County's third courthouse, the Centenary Methodist Church and the fountain made for a very scenic postcard in 1910.

The home of Ben Allen Thomas I was completed in 1900. In the foreground are two women, Yeba Thomas and her sister-in-law Mrs. W. J. "Aunt Mary" Thomas who raised young B. A. Thomas II after his mother's death. To their right is a daughter of Yeba Thomas.

Workmen lay the track for the Interurban.

Faculty members at the old Shelby Graded School on College Street included seated, left to right, Prof. Logan, Prof. Sampson, Angie Willis, Kathleen Kirk, and Ora Hunt; standing, Lillie Hedges, Virginia Bird, Ola Figg, Willie Harbison, Mary Blakemore, Sallie Tevis, and Rose Randolph.

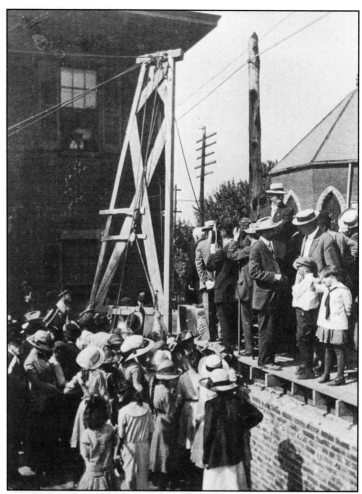

The ladies and the men all wore hats when the current Shelby County courthouse was dedicated in 1913.

World War I was still raging in Europe in September 1918 when these Shelby County men gathered at Camp Mead in Maryland. Standing are Roscoe Webb, Clay Cornelius, _____ Davidson, William Ethington, Arthur Radcliff and Orval Florence; kneeling are Salem Redman, Shelby Sharp, Walter Morgan, Roy McMullen, Herbert Neal, Horace Pearce, and Eddie Mullins; seated are Fred Harrington, Cecil Money, Judiah Gill, George E. Hanser, Caldwell Bird, Guy Duvall, and Edwin Coots.

Historic Cross Keys Inn, shown here in 1921, was known far and wide for its fine food and accommodations. The Marquis de Lafayette dined at Cross Keys in 1825 during his triumphant return to America. His assistance had been vital to the American cause during the Revolutionary War. The historic structure burned to the ground in 1934.

Shelbyville's first Coca-Cola bottling plant stood at 621 Clay Street in 1921. Three other plants were to follow.

Henry G. Cleveland, left, was the manager and his assistant at the Piggly Wiggly store on Main Street in Shelbyville.

Ex-World War I Shelby County soldiers were hired by the local Coca-Cola plant to deliver the soft drink after the war. This vehicle served as a "float" in Shelbyville's 1922 Fourth of July parade.

Shannon Funeral Home, then located at 8th and Main Streets, served the community with this impressive line-up of motor cars. The second car in the line is a "Henny Hearse."

John B. Slucher owned and drove the first school bus in Shelby County. He was the father of Oakley Slucher who was a member of the school board when Shelby County High School was built.

The post office staff at the 6th Street location included left to right, Mrs. Robinson, Mr. McGrath, Mr. Crabster, Mr. Van West, John Meehan, Jones Tribble, Mr. Lynch, Mr. Scofield, Orrin Todd, Roy Money, Roy Money's father, Rodman Hansborough, George Morgan, Mr. Adams, Henley Middleton, and Harry Hastings.

Bidders gathered in 1930 for a tobacco sale at Farmers Tobacco Warehouse (later the Globe Tobacco Warehouse) between 11th and Kentucky Streets. W. Henry Maddox is at right rear standing above and behind the others; Lucien Harbison is at the far right, wearing a bow tie; Sam Skinner is the tallest man at left of center in profile wearing a hat. The warehouse was owned by Roe Williams, Fielding Ballard, J. C. Ray, W. T. Miller, and Ross Shipman.

Jack Frazier and Robert Brammer stand by the first hammer mill in Shelby County in 1933.

Riester & Company store operated for more than 50 years at Finchville. Pictured are Leo Riester, Alberta R. Yancey and Paul Riester.

Interurban car 107 was on its final run from 2nd Street in Shelbyville, where the turntable was located, to Louisville in 1934. The Interurban had reached the fairgrounds in 1910 and downtown Shelbyville in 1912. The popularity of automobiles and improved roads doomed the Interurban which for more than 20 years served Shelby County's passenger and freight needs. The tracks were left until World War II when they were removed and sold as scrap metal to help the war effort.

Brig. Gen. Henry H. Denhardt was gunned down at the intersection of 6th & Main Streets on September 20, 1937, by the three Garr brothers in revenge for the alleged murder of their sister, Verna Garr Taylor, on Nov. 6, 1936, near LaGrange, Kentucky. Gen. Denhardt was on the eve of a second trial for Mrs. Taylor's murder, the first trial ending in a 7-5 vote for acquittal.

The beautiful brunette Verna Garr Taylor of Oldlham County.

The three Garr brothers, Jack, Dr. E. S., and Roy. Only Roy was tried and aquitted for Gen. Denhardt's murder, as Dr. E. S. Garr had been committed to a sanitarium following the shooting, and Jack had not been carrying a weapon at the time of the crime.

A large crowd gathered outside the Armstrong Hotel following the shooting of Gen. Denhardt.

The first man kneeling on the left is Staff Sergeant and waist gunner Edmund Myles with the crew of "Plates Date" in 1943. The four-engine Liberator bomber flew 31 missions from its station in Halesworth, England.

Born in Spencer County in 1882 (his family moved to Shelby County in 1886), attorney and politician Ralph Waldo Emerson Gilbert found fame as a Shelby County judge, five-term U. S. congressman, and Kentucky State legislator. He died in 1939 in the midst of campaigning for the office of Lieutenant-governor.

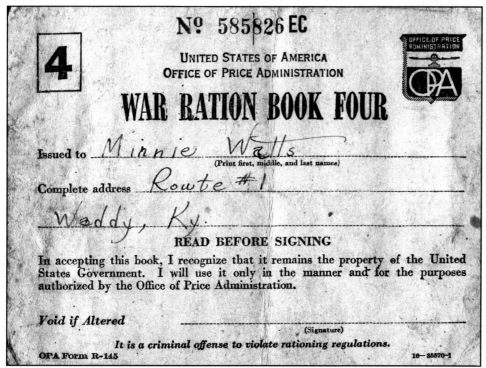

During World War II, nearly every home in Shelby County had a War Ration Book. This one was issued to Minnie Watts of Route 1, Waddy in 1943.

Shelbyville High School's most famous athlete Jack Green blocked a punt as the Red Devils upset Lexington Henry Clay, 14-7, in the 1941 Tobacco Festival game. Later, he would captain the unbeaten national champion Army teams of 1944 and 1945 and be elected to college football's Hall of Fame. He was named head coach at Vanderbilt University in 1963 and served as assistant coach at Kansas and Baylor. He died in 1981. He was one of 10 children of D. L. and May Green, for whom a new bridge was dedicated on the Eminence Pike in 2005.

John Gregory Biagi, son of Annibale and Alberta Biagi, was killed in 1945 by German rifle fire just a few days before the end of World War II. He was an outstanding 1944 graduate of Shelbyville High School. Biagi was one of 57 Shelby County servicemen who died during the conflict. Pvt. Arvil Yeary, son of Mr. and Mrs Neal Yeary, was the first Shelby County boy to lose his life in the war. He was killed in action in the South Pacific.

The tobacco festival in the 1930s, 40s, 50s, and 60s was a major event for many years in Shelbyville, highlighted by a parade, banquet, football game, and street dance. This group gathered in one of the warehouses to help celebrate the occasion.

Dudley Hayes Bottom, front row, far right, and his U.S. Marine Corps buddies display a captured Japanese flag during World War II. Dudley was 18 when he joined the Marines in 1943. He saw action at both Saipan and Iwo Jima. His son, Dudley Jr., was a longtime employee of Shelby Energy Cooperative, retiring as Chief Executive Officer in 2006.

The soldier in the middle in 1944 is Woodrow Wilson Bramblett who, along with his mates, displays a captured Swastika-decorated German flag in 1944.

The Shelby Theatre on the south side of the street between 6th and 7th Streets was the place to be any night of the week during the 1940s and 50s. Note the two gentlemen standing by a parking meter on the right.

Many Shelby County families stopped for a snack or dinner at the Half-Way House about six miles east of Shelbyville on U. S. 60. It was also the "in" place for athletic teams returning from an away game.

President Harry S. Truman, Democrat, spoke to a large crowd of Shelby Countians during his "whistle stop" train trip across America in the summer and fall of 1948. He was introduced by County Judge Coleman Wright. Hundreds of Shelby County school children were bussed to the L & N train station at North 8th Street to hear the man who would go on to defeat Republican Thomas E. Dewey in the November election.

The original Waddy Christian Church and several businesses were destroyed by fire in 1951.

The final freight train on the Shelbyville-Bloomfield line passed through Shelbyville on October 10, 1952.

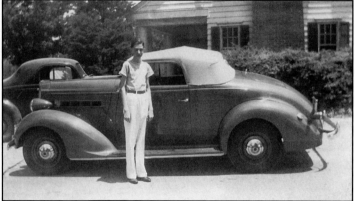

Beverly Randolph, son of Mr. and Mrs. Charles Randolph, was a familiar figure in the 1940s and 50s in his 1937 Packard soft-top convertible.

Left: Whitney M. Young Sr. delivered the remarks to the Lincoln Institute graduating class of 1956-57. Young, who became president of the Institute in 1935, also served as coach and teacher. His son, Whitney M. Young Jr. became a nationally-recognized civil rights figure and headed up the Urban League for many years. President Lyndon Johnson presented Whitney Young Jr. with the Freedom Medal in 1969. He died in a swimming accident near Lagos, Nigeria in 1971.

Shelbyville's most famous businessman and native son, Mark J. Scearce, center, established Wakefield-Scearce Galleries as a pre-eminent antique attraction which enjoys national recognition. Longtime employee Evelyn Flood Hardesty is on the right.

Dr. Charles Elsey was pastor of Shelbyville's First Baptist Church for 31 years. He also wrote a history of the church spanning the years from 1819 to 1962. From 1921 to 1925 he served as the president of Cumberland College at Williamsburg, Kentucky. Brother Elsey died in 1964.

The Mt. Moriah Baptist Church was a thriving church in 1958.

Martha Layne Collins, Kentucky's first and only woman governor, is a native of Bagdad. She served as lieutenant governor from 1979 to 1983, and as governor from 1983 to 1987.

One of seven children and the first in his family to attend college, Willie Fleming attended Shelbyville Junior High School and Lincoln Institute where he was a class of 1947 valedictorian. He attended Fisk University in Tennessee where he graduated with honors, earning a degree in business administration and a minor in history. In 1951 Fleming, along with Alfred Calloway, were the first African-Americans to attend the University Of Louisville School Of Law. He graduated in 1954 with a law degree and in 1955 he passed the Kentucky Bar Exam. Fleming was among several local African-American leaders who helped fully integrate the city swimming pool in the early 1960s. He was also the first local African-American to develop a subdivision, Monica Gardens, named after his oldest daughter, Monica.

Col. Harland Sanders, founder of Kentucky Fried Chicken, presents the keys to a new Dodge van to Gene Hall who directed the Colonel's Mandolin Band of Finchville.

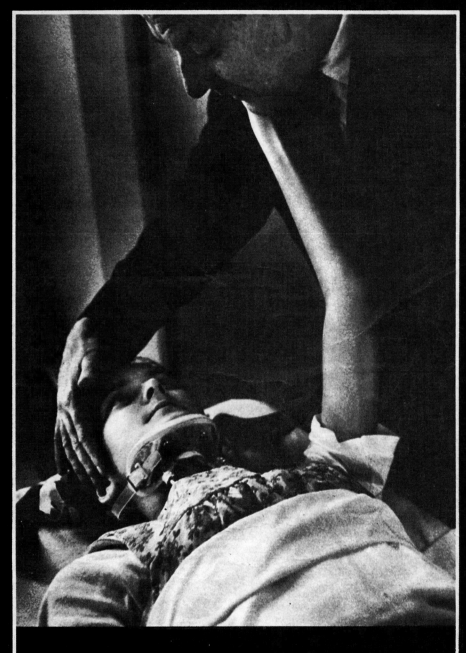

The Courier-Journal & Times
MAGAZINE
SUNDAY, SEPTEMBER 29, 1968

THE VICTIMS OF AUTO ACCIDENTS: Many die and many others must fight for a meaningful life.

A courageous Duanne Puckett appeared on the front cover of *The Louisville Courier-Journal & Times* Sunday magazine section in 1968. Her spinal cord was severed when the car in which she was riding was rear-ended by a drunken driver. Here she is comforted by her father, Jesse Puckett. The photo essay that accompanied the photo was prepared by Bill Strode.

PEOPLE

Lula Morgan Shannon shows off her wedding dress in 1884 at the age of 16.

Several of Waddy's most prominent businessmen in the 1890s included back row, Will Arrington, George Gilpin, Harve Campbell, Col. Joe Snider (USA), and Charles McCormack; middle row, Judd Melear, George Barrigan, Jake Proctor, and John Ben Young; front row, Boyd Hancock and Landon Bailey.

Mark Hardin was the founder of Grove Hill Cemetery.

Shelbyville business men who were moving the city forward at the turn of the 20th century were back row, J. Guthrie Goodman, Eugene Cowles, Hardin Caldwell, George Chowning; front, Mr. Knollenberg, Will McGrath, and T. J. Baldwin.

Other well-known citizens included standing, Charles Lewis, editor of *The Shelby News*, and R. Lee Shannon, undertaker; and, seated, James Bright, tobacco man, and Judge R. Frank Peak, judge of the 6th Judicial District.

Many Shelbyville buildings may be traced back to the architectural genius of Lewis Henry Gruber, as he appeared in the 1890s.

L. H. Gruber's two sons, Lynn Thomas Gruber, left, and Henry Calvin Gruber, right. The man standing is not identified.

Famed astronomer Edwin Hubble lived on Bland Avenue in 1910.

Two generations of the Roemmele families gathered in 1905. Sitting in front are Edith Roemmele Gibbs and Frances Roemmele Lawrence; standing, father Pius Roemmele, his wife Elizabeth Galahue Roemmele, Lillian Roemmele, Agnes Roemmele (the Bohn's mother), and Mr. Fielding Ballard. The house was known as the Old Owen House which burned down while workmen were burning off the old paint. Logs were found under the weather board.

The Carl F. Hanser family came together for this photo in the early 1900s. In the front row are Sally, George Eugene, Elsie, Clara, and Sophie; the parents Carl and Salomie are seated with Robert in between; back row, Bertha, Julia, William, Emily, Otto, Ida and Rudolph.

Vestina Bailey Thomas (1894-1984) in her childhood finery. She married Ben Allen Thomas II on January 25, 1919.

J. M. Hackworth (center) and his six sisters. Standing; Rev. and Mrs. (Helen) Jones, G. S. and Mrs. Amanda Wright. Sitting; Mrs. Elizabeth Logan, Mrs. Sue Hedden, Mrs. Maranda Barriger, and Mrs. Kate Ware.

Finchville provided the backdrop for William Dale and Nancy Stout in 1911.

Will C. Hanna and his sister Lizzie Belle Hanna.

The John Fawkes family included left to right, Clara, Susie, Allie, Boy John, John Sr., Bess and Pauline.

Mr. and Mrs. Julius Albert Porter.

Leven Crafton, grandfather of Tony Carriss, served his country during World War I.

Cam Ballard, on the left, and his friends provided the background music for the silent movies at Layson Hall, at the southeast corner of 7th and Main Streets in Shelbyville.

Betsy Calloway Hanna (Schmidt) and Sophia Lisle Hanna (Castleman Harrison)

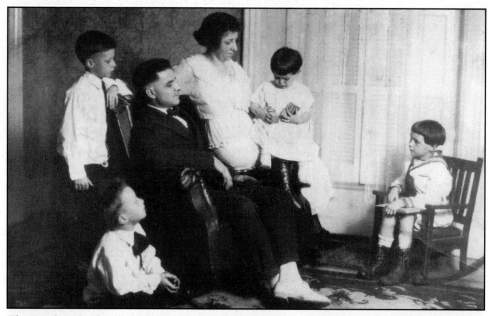

The Frank Bohn family included Marion Bohn (sitting on the floor), standing Paul Bohn, his father Frank and mother Agnes, Mary Agnes and Frank Bohn.

William L. Shannon enjoys riding a pony held by George Gill in 1922. Shannon Funeral Home at 8th & Main Streets provides the background.

Pius Roemmele and his wife Elizabeth, with their four children; Lillian, Agnes (Bohn), Frances R. Lawrence, and Edith R. Gibbs.

Craig Richard Schmidt holds Calvin Tafel Schmidt in the mid-1920s.

William Henry Long and David Tyler Long, sons of D. T. and Corine Long, were photographed in the early 1920s.

Dr. Charles Palmer, local veterinarian, does some hunting in the Mississippi Delta on a plantation owned by Jane Shannon Heath in the 1930s.

Also on a hunting trip in Mississippi were left to right, Charles Randolph, Mandeville Richmond, Paul Long, R. L. Shannon, and Dr. Charles Palmer.

William L. Shannon, Angus Gordon, and Benton Miller listen attentively in 1931 at the Boy Scout Camp at Camp Covered Bridge in 1931.

The Harrisonville Post Office in 1933 was staffed by Dell and Sue Cook. Their children included Margaret Ann and Bettie Sue Cook.

The world's tallest person, Robert Wadlow came to Shelbyville and held David Waide Hughes, with David's mother, Zeleen, looking on. Wadlow was 8' 11" and he wore a size 37AA shoe.

Mary Jane (Molly) Chester Watts is shown here with three of her grandchildren, including Catherine Jane Watts, Doris Moffett, and Raymond B. Watts.

This farm family consisted of left to right, Mrs. Mary Porter, Mary, Hallie, Herbert, Bessie, Ruby and James.

Lucille Eddie Hall shows off Kittie Mae McDonald at the View Point Farm on U.S. 60 in 1938. The horse was owned by her father, B. P. Eddie.

A house on the Dover Road serves as the backdrop for this group which includes back row, Effie Howser Rutledge, Mary Parker Rutledge, Sam Rutledge Jr., Sam Rutledge Sr. and Pattie Bush Rutledge. In the front are Philip Rutledge Jr. and Davis Rutledge Burk.

Bob, Howard, and Bill Logan, sons of Mr. and Mrs. Lindsey Logan, have that serious look in the 1930s.

Dr. John Foree Jesse, photographed here in 1939, served the citizens of Waddy during his long tenure as a family physician.

James and Eleanor Burnett were congratulated by this group on their wedding day, Dec. 30, 1941. In the front row are Morton Berry, Robert Connor, Dolly Connor, and Frances Berry; back row, Eleanor, James, Dean Burnett and Burdick Burnett.

Burgess Parks was a longtime coach and principal at Cropper High School.

Robert B. Gaines served his country during WWII. This photo was taken in 1943.

Ensign Neal Hammon served his country during World War II, later becoming a successful architect and Kentucky historian.

Captain Tyler Long, center, on duty here in 1942, was one of more than 1580 men and women from Shelby County who served their country during World War II.

Waddy Homemakers the early 1940s. First row, left to right; Mrs Jim Jetter (holding grandson Bobby Shouse), Mrs. Sara Snider, Mrs. Jeanie Ireland, Mrs. Mae Snider, Mrs. Josie Cook; back row, left to right; Mrs. Bertha Skelton, Mrs. Rose Tucker, Miss Billie Brown, Mrs. Maggie Johnson. Mrs. Pearl Cook, Mrs. Nell Shouse, Mrs King, Mrs. Hattie McCormack, and Mrs. Carrie Cook.

A pioneer in the development of the local rural electric cooperative was William E. Dale (1894-1950).

Anna Lee Hardesty and Lucille Eddie get ready to cheer for Shelbyville High School.

Forrest Smith poses with his daughter Mary Lou in the mid-1940s.

Nancy Durrett, Betty Robinson, and Lillian Woods in 1945.

Freddy, Jesse, and Bobby Baxter posed for this photo with their brother Tommy in front.

Elmo and Nancy Ethington gathered Easter eggs in 1948.

In the late 1940s these Cub Scouts included seated, Fielding Ballard, Henry Mathis, and Cam Scearce; standing, Edgar "Bub" Gibson, Tommy Thompson, Hite Hays, Charles Bradbury, Mike Simpson, and Ralph S. Mitchell. Thompson was killed in Vietnam during the early years of that war.

The David Tyler Long family in 1949 included left to right, Charles Thomas Long, David Marshall Long, Edith Marshall Long, David Tyler Long, and Robert Tyler Long.

The Bowles gathered for a family outing in the 1940s at the family farm near Cropper. From left to right are John Paul Martin, Gladys (Bowles) Martin, George Thomas Bowles, Myrtle (Truax) Bowles, Buddy Bowles (standing in front of his mother), Roy Lee Bowles, Virginia Bowles Jennings, and Wilbert Jennings.

Phyllis, Lula M., Jane, and Peggy Ann Shannon are pictured in the parlor of Mr. and Mrs. R. Lee Shannon's home in 1949.

Moses Ruben owned Ruben's women's clothing store in Shelbyville for many years and endowed a trust fund which has given away many thousands of dollars to worthy Shelby County causes.

Ben Allen Thomas II was a leader in agriculture, tobacco and dairy cooperatives. He managed the family farm, Chenoweth Farm, for 40 years.

Lucy Hall (Long) and her father Edwin W. Hall were enjoying the Shelby County Fair in 1950.

The Jesse Puckett family in 1950 included Jesse and his wife Eula, and their three daughters, Marsha, Duanne, and Terry.

B.P. Eddie was a prominent tobacco farmer and citizen.

85 years span this group which includes Ben Gaines Matthews, Benjamin Franklin Matthews, Robert Foster Matthews Sr. and Robert F. Matthews Jr. Mr. Matthews Sr. is holding Charles Killgore Matthews, born in 1950, the first child of Bob Jr. and Betty Matthews. His great-grandfather, B. F. Matthews was born in 1865.

Louise Catlett and J. B. Whitten are having fun in 1950.

Edgar Vaughan, Ben Pollard, and Willard Igleheart showed off their fishing skills in 1952 while on a Boy Scout trip to Canada.

The choir of the Cropper Christian Church in 1922 included first row, organist Rose Shaw, Marjorie Price, Amelia Prather, Eunice Roberts, May Wood, Mary Quenette, Mildred Chandler, Mary Blanch Kelly, Bessie Tipton, and Ruth Long; second row, Paul Wells, Everett Shaw, and Linnie Shaw.

One of Shelby County's most distinguished families included front row, left to right, Fanny Roland, Ella Roland, Oliver Roland Sr. holding Roland Dale, Willie Roland, Christine Roland, Corky Clemons; back row, left to right, Lura Roland Jr., Oliver Roland Jr., Dollie Roland, Doloris Clemons, Orantes Roland, Lura Roland Sr., and Mark Clemons.

Col. R. R. Van Stockum, far right, was the presiding officer when Senior Flag and General Officers of the Far East Command held services for the Unidentified Dead of the Korean War at Yokosuka Navy Yard, in Japan on January 20, 1956.

Nancy Finney was interviewed on WHAS by Milton Metz.

Dr. and Mrs. Wayne Ward

James and Mary Ellen Hackworth are proud of their grandsons, David, John, and Neil.

The Shelbyville Rotary Club celebrated its 25th anniversary in 1952. On hand for the occasion were, unidentified, longtime club secretary-treasurer Judge Coleman Wright, Horace Cleveland, and Mark Scearce.

In the 1950s the Shelbyville Rotary Club planted, cultivated and sold a small allotment of tobacco as a club fund-raiser. Taking the crop to market were, among others, Rotarians Briggs Lawson, Judge Coleman Wright, Auldon Edwards, Guthrie Goodman Jr., and Roy Ratcliff.

At one time the Masons had four sets of twins. They included the Ramsey, Newby, Riggs, and Williams brothers.

This 1950s group from the Methodist Church Friendship Class includes left to right: Paul and Grace Hardesty, Lynn Miller, Morris Bryant, Helen Cleveland, Joseph and Mary Anderson Burks, Bonnie and Jim Merchant, Katherine Cleveland, Eugene and Martha Stewart, Ada Carter, Pauline Adams, Lucille Smith, and Charles Adams.

The Shelbyville Kiwanis Club harvested a small crop of tobacco as a fund-raising venture in the 1950s. In the front, left to right, are Lynn Miller, Clarence Catlett, and Melvin Sams Jr.

George Ann Carpenter was for many years a revered teacher in the Shelbyville city schools. She also served as school librarian and was a well-known local historian and re-enactor.

The Briggs Lawson family included Briggs Adams, Lettie Lawson (on floor), Murray and Briggs Lawson, Gregg Adams, and Hays Lawson; back row: Bill and Cecie Adams, Sydney and Bobby Lawson.

Charles Adams, his son Paul Morgan and mother Esther Adams preparing for a motorcycle outing.

This group of youngsters enjoyed an outing to Camp Bingham in 1955. In the front row are Judy Ware, Charlotte Hardin, Judy Lea, Paul Fry, Allen Bailey, and Phil Bland; the back row includes Barbara Wallace, Katherine Lea, John Thompson, Donnie Bramblett, Dickie Trammel, Billy Wallace, James Clark, Mrs. Paul Fry, Ronnie Bland, and Jerry Trammel.

Dorothy Mills is proud of her family, including, left, Annette, Emmett, Dorothy, Ben, Bill and Pam.

Rufus Harrod and his scout troop. Holding flag, left to right; Danny Hall and Buster Stanley; standing, left to right; Rufus Harrod, Benton Kinsolving, Virgil Wheeler, Johnny Hall, Roy Bailey, Melvin Layle Sams, Johnny Harrod.

Tony Carriss and his sister Vivian with their parents, Jay and Bessie Mae Carriss in 1957.

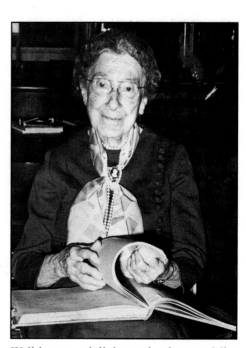

Well-known violinist and educator Miss Harriett Poynter was for many years an instructor at Science Hill School.

Alex B. Veech of Finchville was an early promoter of rural electrification and a prominent figure in agriculture.

Miss Juliet Poynter served as the overseer of Science Hill School for many years.

Daisy Saffell, the first wife of George Saffell, became the first African-American woman in Kentucky to obtain her embalmer's and undertaker's licenses. The Saffells opened a funeral home in 1909 at the corner of 9th and Clay Streets and, at that time, this was the only funeral home where African-Americans could hold a wake for their loved ones. She had a local hospital on 10th Street named after her. She died in 1918.

The J. Hayden Igleheart family in 1958 included bottom, left to right: Gladys, Margaret and Eloise; second row, Gladys Houtchens Igleheart, J. Hayden Igleheart, Sadie Payne Igleheart, Debby, and Jamie; third row, Betty Rees Igleheart, Susie Gillock, Louise Rees Igleheart, Willard Igleheart, J. Hayden Igleheart, Jr; fourth row, Elliot Igleheart, Julian Igleheart, Ted and Libby Igleheart.

Jane Glenn Hardin's birthday party in 1958. Standing, left to right; Linda Caldwell, Sarabeth Chatham, Amy Harris, Ann Stanley, Jane Glenn Hardin, Brenda Yancey, Dora Lawrence, Nancy Shannon, Jane Shannon.; middle row, left to right; Katherine Kinsolving, Judy Swindler, Wendy Caldwell, Rose Guthrie, Cecie Pearce; front; Bette Harris.

Renowned concert pianist Betty Jean Chatham not only played the organ at the First Baptist Church for many years, but traveled worldwide on behalf of the gospel and made many recordings of her music.

The family of Jack Lawson included left to right, Stanley, Eve, Evelyn, Addie (Jack's aunt), Jack, Mrs. Stanley Lawson (Jack's mother), Lyle, and Kenny. Stanley was killed in Vietnam in the early years of the conflict.

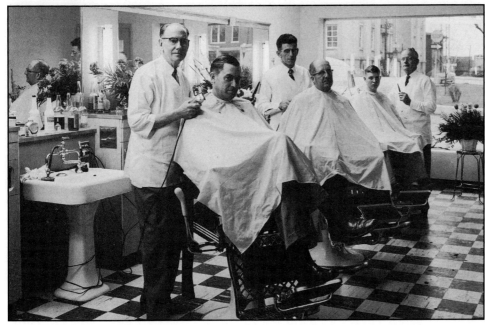

Cleveland's Barber Shop was a favorite locale for the men, young and old. This group includes left to right, Charlie Cleveland, Arnold Hawkins, Delbert Black, Police Chief Roy S. Jones, David Crombie, and Virgil Carpenter.

Howard Streible presents the "Optimist of the Year" award to Harold Major, who also served as the club's president.

Left to right; Charles Long, Lamar Hundley, Curtis Hardesty, Scott Miller, Hunt Garner, Billy Anderson, Monty Montgomery, Edgar Fullenwider, and Guthrie Thompson.

Howard and Mary Pearce on Magnolia Avenue in Shelbyville, probably in 1948. Among those present were Lucille Shuck Pearce, Jack Pearce, Clifford Pearce, Luther Pearce, Ted Pearce, Walter "Dee" Huddleston, Philip Pearce, Bob Pearce, Frank Pearce, Howard Pearce, Charles Anderson, Julia Pearce, Kathleen Pearce Anderson, Leona Pearce, Margaret Pearce Wilhoite, Jackie Lee Pearce, Charleen Anderson, Peggy Pearce, Kitty Anderson, and Jean Pearce Huddleston. The three missing Pearce siblings are Mamie Pearce Clove, Horace Pearce, and Clay Pearce.

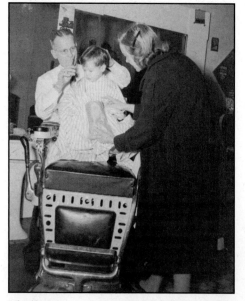

Virgil Carpenter gives Mike McGinnis his first haircut.

In 1949 four generations of the Kemper family.

The Mathis family included front row, left to right, Ben, Henry, Fred Lea, John, and Sally Mathis; second row, Edith (holding Sallie Mathis), Lewis Mathis Jr, Doris Goodnight, Margaret Mathis Goodnight, John F. Mathis, Catherine Mathis Jett, and Christine Mathis; back row, David, William T., Lewis Mathis Sr., and Mary Stuart Mathis; William M. Goodnight next to his father William Goodnight, Jeptha Jet, and Fred Mathis Sr.

Coonskin caps obviously appealed to these Hackworth youngsters. From left to right are John, David (on bike), and Neil.

Jim, Lucinda, Lamar and Howard Hundley were the children of Lamar and Clarty Hundley.

Mrs. Laura R. Young was the wife of Dr. Whitney Young who ran Lincoln Institute for 35 years. Mrs. Young was also the first African-American postmaster in Kentucky.

Prominent Shelbyville businessman Mark J. Scearce operated a jewelry store on Main Street for many years before opening Wakefield-Scearce Galleries in the early 1960s.

Neil Hackworth's birthday party included front row: Tim Finn, Alice Amyx, Pres Hall, C.L. Burk; second row: Lucinda Hundley, Lamar Hundley, Ann Miller, Rose Malcolm Davis, Bob Montgomery, Margaret Eggen, Jean Wood, Neil Hackworth, Edgar Fullenwider, Scott Miller, Bill Long, Doug Swindler, Eddie Crossfield, Molly Webb; third row: John Allen Estes, Rusty Brown, Grant Hays, Charles Black, Van Underwood. Couch: Guthrie Thompson, Ruth Wood (grandmother), Dorothy Wood (aunt), David Hackworth (brother), James Hackworth (father), and Mary Ellen Hackworth (mother).

Jim Heady Wakefield partnered with Mr. Scearce in the Wakefield-Scearce Galleries.

Amos Porter and Al Miller work on the counter weight for the partition at the Methodist Church.

The Fielding Ballard family included front, left to right: Linda (Humston) Knight, Barbara Shelby Scearce (Mrs. Mike Boyd), Linn (Pierce), Stan Pierce, III, Fielding E. Ballard, Sr., Hattie W. Ballard, Mark Ballard, Leonard H. Ballard, Ed Humston, Jr., Fielding E. Ballard, III; second row, left to right: Cecie Scearce (Mrs. J. Chewning), Elizabeth Ballard, Harriet Ballard (Mrs. Roger Butterbaugh), Susan Scearce (Mrs. Pat Burnett), Joyce (Mrs. Jack) Pierce, Susan Ballard (Mrs. Charles Humston, Sr.), Helen (Mrs. Fielding E.) Ballard, Jr., Pat Ballard, Cam Scearce, Gaile (Mrs. Charles) Humston, Jr., holding Becky (Humston) Gash; back row, left to right, Mark J. Scearce, Peytie Ballard (Mrs. Mark J. Scearce), Dr. Edward N Humston, Donna Lea (Mrs. Edward N Humston), William A. Scearce, Jr., J. Stanton Pierce, Victorine Ballard (Mrs. J. Stanton Pierce), Ballard Pierce, Jack Pierce Stanton, Jr., Charles Humston, Sr., Victorine Weakley (Mrs. Philemon Bird), Cam W. Ballard, Jean (Mrs. Cam) Ballard, Fielding E. Ballard, Jr., Peggy (Mrs. Leonard W.) Ballard, Harriet Ballard (Mrs. William A. Scearce), William A. Scearce, Sr., Judy Scearce, Leonard W. Ballard, and Charles Humston, Jr.

The Dr. K. E. Ellis family included bottom, left to right Debbie, Emma, Larry, and Kennett; standing, James, Janelda, Kennett, and Marlene.

Clara Cleveland, prize winning baker of cakes, provided Shelbyville with many birthday and special occasion cakes for many years.

This fashion show at Southside Elementary features Mary Brainard Bell, Mona Brown, Rosella Yeager Cunningham Davis, Helen Tichenor Montgomery, and Susie Clemmons Saunders.

This local band "Guy and the Gifters" includes Guy Shelburn, Benjie Mathis, John Cleveland, and Larry Tinnel.

The members of another local band "The Optical Illusion" are Bill Ray Baker, Eddie Meeks, Vance Reister, Danny Hauck, and Paul Morgan Adams.

Joseph and Mary Anderson Burks in 1963 were obviously proud of their family which included front, Paul, Mark and John; standing, Bonnie, Carl David, and Joey.

Charles and Bernice Graybill take a moment to relax among his dahlias, for which he was known statewide.

The George E. Hanser family included left to right, Katherine Hanser Tingle, George E. Hanser, Vern Mirre, G. A. Mirre, Mary Kinser Hanser, Katie Huffman Kinser, Andy Walbeck, and Julia Kinser Walbeck.

On July 2, 1962, Susanne Van Stockum helps U. S. Marine Commandant David Shoup pin the stars of a Brigadier General on the shoulders of her husband, Ronald R. Van Stockum.

In 1960 Robert F. and Zerelda B. Matthews (seated in center) gathered with their six grandchildren at the family home at 1108 West Main. In the front are Gaines, Blair, Beau, Alan, Charlie, and Lisa Gaines Matthews; standing are Else, Bill, Jean, Betty, and Ben Matthews.

Enjoying a fishing trip to Curtain Falls, Canada in 1965 were left to right, Robert M. Walters, Lindsey Logan, Paul F. Schmidt, Briggs Lawson, and Mark Scearce. (The photo was taken by Fulton Smith)

Ira and Catherine McKinley's children, Judy Carol, R. T., Jerry and niece Angela Spinks were captured on film in 1966.

The family of Mr. and Mrs. Willie Fleming includes left to right, Denise Hayden, Charles Marshall, Jackie Fleming, Mr. Fleming, Kim Carter, Yonzel Fleming, and Monica Ferguson.

Methodist minister and Air Force Chaplin William E. Hisle.

Brothers Joe, Cecil, and Paul Stapleton.

Four generations of the William Andriot family. Standing are Bill Jr. with daughter Toni; sitting, Mattie and William Andriot Sr., and Rob Carter.

Left to right are Betsy Adams (McClain), Alice Richardson, Rita Whitaker (Kanzinger), Lucille Fry (Grey), Leona Waits in car driven by Ronnie Miller represent the Shelby Boat and Ski Club.

This group of youngsters going to conservation camp at Camp Currie in 1964 include Danny Hauck, Harry Hardesty, Tom Hardesty, John Snider, Mark Ballard, Ronnie Bottom, Laury Baker, Lowry Miller, Joe Frazier, Jim Cleveland, Paul Joplin all from Shelbyville; Paul Long and Keith Long of Cropper; Rodney Murphy, Gordon McGuire and Ray Travis of Mt. Eden; James West of Bagdad; Evan Arms and Lee Bryant of Finchville; and Gary Jones, Robert Giltner, David Scearce, and Robbie Marshall of Gleneyrie.

The family of D.L. and May Green gathered in 1968. Mr. and Mrs. Green had 10 children.

Sallie Demaree Petty was a familiar figure in downtown Shelbyville for many years.

Stewart Demaree, left, posed with Nathalia and Louis Ruben, and Bill Shannon at Solomon Lodge 5.

Long-time Kiwanians at the club's 40th anniversary celebration included seated, Everett Hall; standing, left to right: Charles Graybill, Rufus Harrod, Jesse Puckett, and Carl Bryant.

Mr. and Mrs. James Scofield were recognized for their services to the community in 1971. Benny Lanter, who ran a grocery for many years at the corner of 10th & College Streets, made the presentation.

Dr. A. L. Birch, local veterinarian, is shown in a 1973 photograph as he gave a rabies vaccine to a milk cow on the J. R. Sanderlin farm after several rabid foxes were killed on area farms. Dr. Birch vaccinated 500 cows in the Sanderlin herd.

Siblings of the John William Long family gathered left to right: Sarah Sharp, Mary Katherine Jackson, Nancy Stout, Tom Long, Frank Long, Lowry Ingram, and Anna Stapleton.

Roy Stephen Bruner, Donna K. Gaines Bruner and their son David Wayne Bruner in 1975.

Bill Amyx is named Shelbyville Postmaster.

Robert Larry Gaines in 1974.

Ben Thomas, Ted Thomas, John Graham, and Charles Hedges spent the summer of 1975 repairing barns on Chenoweth Farm.

Daphne and Alvin Ethington in 1976.

In 1976 the children of Betsy and Robert Megibben; standing, Garry; middle, Hart and John; front, Michael.

John and Pearl Durrett pose with their great-grandchildren, Shane Suttor and Camm Suttor, in 1977.

Col. Harland Sanders photographed here with Robert Montgomery, son of Helen Tichenor Montgomery.

The Edward Hayes family; seated, Edward and Shirley Hayes and daughter Katherine Bryant; standing, daughters Ann Rutledge and Sarah Elizabeth.

The children of Henry Caldwell and Sophia Lisle Bird include standing, left to right, Branch, Philemon, and Stuart Bird, Lisle Bird Hanna, and Henry "Harry" Bird; seated are Mary Carlile Bird Bell and Tate Bird.

James R. Price, center, is recognized for his 20 years of service to the Federal Land Bank in 1979. His wife Marjorie joined in the celebration.

The six children of Ed and Anna Warren, center; back row Wanda, Vivian, Barbara, and Joan; in the front are Jeanette and Jennifer.

Anna Warren, Letha Kelley, and Mariah Mack were among community leaders.

The family of Joe Callahan included Avery, Joe, Faye, and Amber.

Stewart and Eleanor McBrayer were popular figures. Both were active in the First Christian Church, and Stewart was president of Citizens Union Bank.

Ann Graham, (holding Hanna), Corinna, and John Graham relax in front of their farm home on Martin Netherly Lane near Mt. Eden in 1977.

Jimmy Hedden was frequently seen bicycling around town and acting as an unofficial traffic officer at minor accidents.

Eleanor and James Burnett were honored when a park, just off Brown Avenue, was dedicated in Jimmy's name on May 5, 1977.

One of Shelby County's many "characters" over the years, Fletcher White always had a ready grin.

The Richard Ellis family included left to right, Stephen Clark Ellis, Becky Curtis Ellis, Ann Michelle Ellis Cloyd, Jeffrey Scott Ellis, Mary Helen Ellis Frazier, Shirley Kemper Ellis, Richard B. Ellis, Melissa Gove Ellis, and Steven Wayne Ellis.

The nine children of Mrs. Juanita (Emzy) Vest Gaines include first row, Paul Ray Gaines, Robert Byron Gaines, Gene Gaines, and J. D. Gaines; second row, Edith Gaines Armstrong, Hazel Gaines Ends, Louise Gaines Garrett, Gladys Gaines Chesher. Louise lived with her mother-in-law, Minnie Garrett, at 627 Main Street. This address now houses the Shelbyville Welcome/Heritage Center.

Virginia and Wayne Bell were instrumental in helping Shelbyville's First Christian Church grow between 1941 and 1951. Rev. Bell later pastored churches in Richmond, Virginia, and Nashville, Tennessee before serving as president of Lexington Theological Seminary.

Louis Ruben, 92, and Charles B. Long were among the long-standing golfers at the Shelbyville Country Club. Ruben was one of the Club's charter members dating back to the 1920s.

Lt. governor Martha Layne Collins greets Tony Carriss in 1980.

Mrs. Florence Van Stockum, mother of General Ronald Van Stockum was born in 1894. When she died in Shelbyville in 2005 at the age of 110, she was listed as the 53rd oldest person in the world, as documented by the Gerontology Research Group.

Photographer John Wesley Williams brought photography to Shelby County in the 1850s.

Many avid Shelby County outdoorsmen gathered at Lake George in Florida in 1980. They included standing, Bernie Graybeal, King Walters, Sid Krieger, Fritz Finger, Calvin Schmidt, Bud English, Bill DuBourg, Bill Griffin, Bill Hundley, Dick Tygrett and Art Barnett; kneeling, Ted Igleheart, Frank Kees, John O'Dell, Harry Moore, Bill Thompson, unidentified, Bryant Barco, Howard Logan, Willie Broughton, and Bob Purnell. Stretched out in front is Neal Hammon.

Peggy Williams Miller photographed here in her uncle Otho Willams portable dark room.

Ellis McGinnis ran a photography business in Shelbyville in the 1940s and 50s. This pose with his wife Evelyn is for a Christmas card.

The family of Dr. and Mrs. Tom Williams includes his brother Otho and daughter Peggy.

Henry and Katherine Cleveland also ran a photography business in the 1950s and 60s. They are captured here by son Jim after completing a wedding assignment.

BUSINESSES

The Glacier Ice Company, founded in 1891, later became the Shelbyville Ice Company.

Bowland & Heaton was an early Shelbyville tinsmith.

Hall & Son Lumber Co. was established in 1891 on 7th Street. It remained in the Hall family until 1992. W. H. Hall was followed by his son, Curtis P. Hall, and later by his son, Edwin W. Hall.

The interior of S. S. Kirk's Grocery Store.

Logan and Logan Flouring Mill as it appeared in 1899.

Hoke & Jesse feed store and stables at the turn of the 20th century.

A dry goods and shoe store side by side on the north side of Main Street, just west of 6th Street and adjoining the Farmers & Traders Bank.

George Thomas Bowles, Lee Bowles, and Tevis Stone appear in this blacksmith shop in Finchville in 1910.

Workers at the Shelby Co. Equity Warehouse gathered for the photographer.

Collecting tobacco was a highly manual operation in 1910.

The original Crescent Roller Mill was one of several mills that operated in Shelby County in the early 1900s.

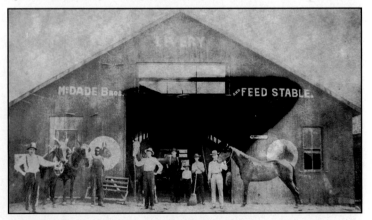

Schooler and Frederick offered farm implements, groceries, and other supplies.

McDade Bros. operated a livery and feed stable.

Layson Hall, located on the southeast corner of 7th & Main Streets, offered many types of entertainment in the early 1900s. This is a picture of the theatre screen

Travis Wilson's Saddle Shop is on the left with his residence adjoining. It was on the north side of Main Street between 4th and 5th Streets. Later, the building would become the store of John M.

In 1915 the Interurban tracks were located in the middle of Main Street.

These men were attending a lecture at the annual tobacco institute.

The Shelby Sentinel, which began as *The Shelby News* in 1840, was owned by Michael O'Sullivan in the early 1920s.

Ed D. Shinnick was the editor and publisher of *The Shelby Record* which also did job printing.

On the left is William C. Shinnick, on the right his brother Ed. D. Shinnick.

Famed photographer John Wesley Williams is seen here in the window of *The Shelby News*.

Climax Roller Mills was a flourishing operation in the early 20th century.

A reminder of the early days in transportation was the old livery stable located at 5th & Washington Streets.

Owen and Moore was located on the south side of the 500 block of Main Street in the early 1920s. Note the sign indicating the skating rink on the second floor.

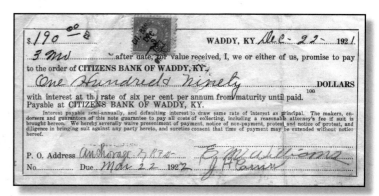

The Citizens Bank of Waddy was charging 6% interest on this note dated Dec. 22, 1921.

The second Coca-Cola plant was built at 2nd and Clay Streets in 1922.

The W. A. Wayne Building was located where Commonwealth Bank & Trust now stands on the south side of Main between 4th and 5th Streets

T. C. Snider was the owner-operator of the Waddy Garage in 1929.

This store was located on the Scott Station Road in the 1920s.

Biagi's was originally a Goodrich tire dealer at the corner of 6th and Washington Streets.

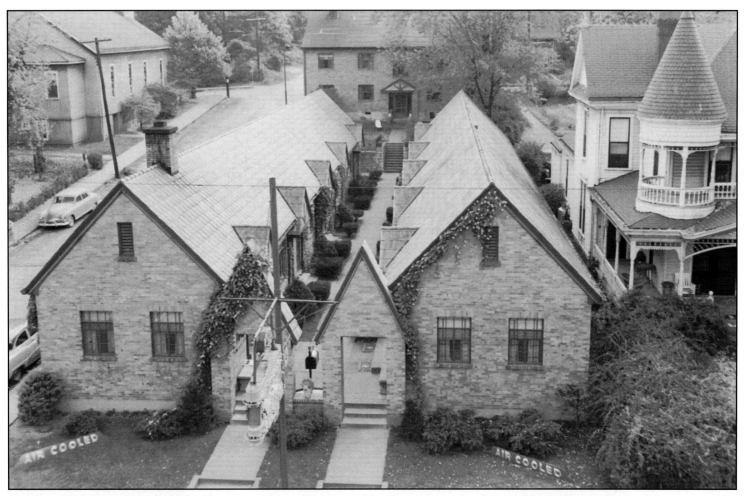

The Blue Gables Motel provided the first central air conditioning and heating system when it opened in the late 1930s.

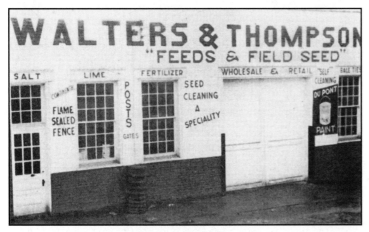

Walters & Thompson was a flourishing feed store on Clay Street in 1949.

Joe Best, second from left, and Dave Eakins, first man on the right, were longtime operators of Shelbyville Welding & Brazing Company.

Rubens Dry Cleaning located on south 6th Street was owned by Louis Ruben.

In 1949 Shelbyville was served by this fleet of Hinkle taxis.

The White Cottage was located between 7th and 8th Streets.

Howser's Appliance Store was located on 6th Street.

Baker & Kasper was located on Main Street between 5th and 6th Streets.

Carl Graybeal operated an auto parts store for many years on east Main Street.

A Desoto dealership stood next to an International Harvester dealership on the north side of 4th Street.

Dinkler's Meats & Vegetables was a well regarded grocery store on east Main Street.

Joe Hayes Chevrolet and a Sinclair service station were located on the south side of Main Street between 7th and 8th Streets.

Logan's Laundry operated for many years from the corner of 10th & Washington Streets.

Kroger originally operated on the north side of the 500 block of Main Street.

Kroger moved to this location next to the Episcopal Church on Main Street in the early 1950s.

The third Coca-Cola plant operated from 1947 to 1974 on east Main Street.

Bryant-Ratcliffe Co. was owned by Carl Bryant and Paul Ratcliffe.

Puckett's Men Store was popular with the young men of the community.

"Tubby" Denton operated a grocery store on Washington Street in the 1950s.

Southern States Shelbyville Cooperative has long served the community from this location on south 7th Street.

This was the scene when the Maple Moo ice cream bar and restaurant opened in 1955.

Later, the Maple Moo became Jerry's Drive-In on U.S. 60 west.

Tracy's was originally located on the south side in the 400 block of east Main Street.

Eggen's Television was on 6th Street

The City Café was located on the north side of the 700 block of Main Street.

Donohue's Motel was located on U. S. 60 west.

Master ice cream maker Frank Bohn checks his work in this photo taken by his son Paul Bohn.

The menu at Bohn's Creamery shows ice cream cones selling for 5 and 10 cents, popsicles 5 cents and sundaes 15 cents.

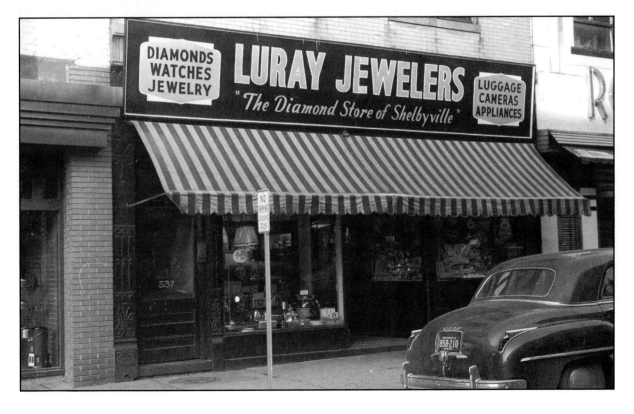

Roy Jochum owned Luray Jewelers on Main Street.

Hall-Taylor originally operated from this location on the north side of Main Street near the railroad tracks.

Charlies Pool Room was one of several pool halls that operated on Main Street for many years.

The Nancy Lou shop was the place to shop for the young people.

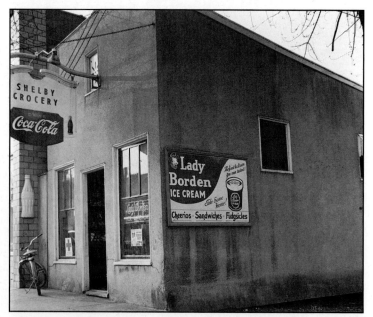

The Shelby Grocery was located on West Main Street between 10th and 11th Streets. Henry Cleveland was the owner.

In 1922 this Italianate Revival house was built for the Slater family at 1185 Main Street. In 2008 it is the Hall-Taylor Funeral Home.

Andriot's Men's Store celebrated its grand opening in the mid-1950s.

Store manager Kenny Mitchell looks on as Aubrey Jones fits Curtis Hardesty with a pair of shoes at Lerman's.

The Shelbyville Candy and Tobacco Company operated from the north side of Main Street between 4th & 5th Streets.

Van's 5 and 10 was a popular store, especially for seeds in the springtime and novelties anytime.

Purnell's "Old Folks" Whole Hog Country Sausage had its modest beginnings at this Simpsonville plant. Now it is a national distributor of pork-related products.

A model for Mary's Frock Shop appears at the Dairy Del in 1956.

Purnell Sausage Company founder Allen Purnell checks a sausage roll.

The Shelby Motel served travelers for many years from its location on U. S. 60 west. It went out of business and was demolished in 2007.

The Prescription Shop in the 600 block of north Main Street was owned by Mr. and Mrs. Kenneth Easley.

Crume-Hundley Oil Company began operating in the 1920s.

Herman Atlas was a well-known citizen and city council member who operated a scrap iron and metals business on south 1st Street. Note his telephone number: 28.

"Doc" Headen, center, operated a service station on the south side of Main Street between 7th and 8th Streets. He received help from Raymond Jesse, left, and Waddy Jesse, right.

Scofield Pharmacy operated one of three soda fountains in downtown Shelbyville.

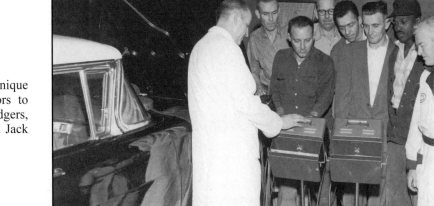

An instructor demonstrated a new technique in auto technology at Pearce Motors to Harold Casey, James Acree, Don Rodgers, Riley Satterwhite, Charles Dale, and Jack Pearce.

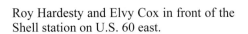

Roy Hardesty and Elvy Cox in front of the Shell station on U.S. 60 east.

The barbers in this photo include left to right, Horace Asay, Paul Jackson, Sidney Hackett, and Bill Crane cutting Dr. Shield's hair.

Biagi's showed off its renovated store at a grand opening in 1954.

Rothchild clothing store operated for more than 90 years on the north side of Main Street between 5th & 6th Streets.

The Reddy Electric Company was one of many businesses located at the corner of 8th and Main Streets. In 2008 the Shelby County Community Theatre stands at this location.

The office and warehouse of the Long Silo and Block Co. were located on south 3rd Street

The Shelby Theatre was flanked by the Southern Dollar Store and a liquor store in 1960.

A number of patrons have enjoyed a show at The Shelby Theatre.

Shelbyville had a bakery on 6th Street.

The Shelby County Trust & Banking Company had its entrance on Main Street for many years.

The Shelby County tobacco market ranked No. 3 in statewide sales for many years. These gentlemen move some of the crop around at the Star Warehouse.

The tobacco auctions generally started in November and concluded in February.

Baskets of tobacco fill the floor at the Big Shelby Warehouse on 7th Street in the 1950s.

The Gulf Oil Station at 10th & Main Streets was a busy place.

The Shelby Office Equipment Company had recently been remodeled when this photo was taken.

The Farmers & Traders Bank stood for many years at the corner of 6th & Main Streets. Note the Ruben's store, operated by Moses Ruben, adjacent to it.

W. P. Deiss sold wallpaper, paint, stationery, and books at his store on Main Street between 5th & 6th Streets.

Cinnamonds General Store provided fresh meats, fruits and vegetables.

Lerman Brothers, along with Lincoln's, was one of Shelbyville's most popular stores for clothing and household wares.

This Ashland station was located on U. S. 60 east at the intersection with Benson Pike.

Mary's Frock Shop was a popular drawing card for the young ladies.

The telephone company office building was at the corner of 8th & Washington Streets.

Wadlington's Hardware store was located on the south side of Main Street between 5th and 6th Streets. Lawson's took over the space when Wadlington's went out of business in the early 1960s.

This interior view of Mark J. Scearce Jewelry Store on Main Street reveals an up-to-date, snazzy appearance.

Mark J. Scearce Jewelry was featuring Elgin watches in this exterior shot.

Rothchild's had a plentiful selection of shoes and several stations to try them on. This location on Main Street later became Briggs-Hower, and later Bistro 535.

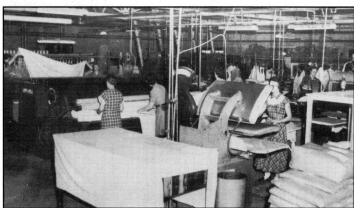

Logan's Laundry was in full operation at the corner of 10th & Washington Streets in the 1950s.

Miss Mabel Oats, who worked at *The Shelby Sentinel* for more than 50 years, shows off the paper to a group of visiting newspaperman from Cuba before the revolution.

Roll Forming began operating on Goodman Avenue in the 1950s.

Lawson's Department Store offered these fashions in a front window display.

Begley Drugs, a Walgreen agency, was located on the south side of Main Street at the intersection with 6th Street.

Harry Long operated the Buick dealership on U.S. 60 west, next to the Fairgrounds, in 1953.

An employee was monitoring the bottling line at the Coca-Cola plant in the 1950s.

Mr. and Mrs. Prentice Kinser Sr. were the original owners of Kinser's Store at 100 North 9th Street.

Davis Motors was selling new cars from this location at the intersection of 5th and Washington Streets. The Shelby County Courthouse Annex is now located on this site.

Nick Riner sold late-model used cars on Main Street between 6th & 7th Streets.

St. Charles Furniture Store occupied the buildings at the intersection of 4th & Main Streets. Ford and Desoto dealerships had once occupied the corner building.

Wakefield-Scearce Galleries represented the creative genius of Mark J. Scearce, with financial assistance from Jim Heady Wakefield.

Bob Fay, foreground, watches the printing of *The Shelby News* on a Vanguard press in the mid-1960s. Dave Harris stands next to Bob. The press was located in the basement of the old A & P building on the south side of Main Street between 5th & 6th Streets.

C. Thomas Craig was noted for his real estate sales and fast-paced auctions. His office was on 6th Street.

Begley's soda fountain was the "in" place for the lunch crowd in the 1960s.

Carriss's Country Store is a long-standing matter of community pride at Southville.

Bobby Stratton operated a grocery and bait shop on U. S. 60 for several years before he became Shelby County judge executive.

The Climax Roller Mills, which started doing business in 1874, was demolished on September 24, 1986.

This is the last home (1974-1994) of Shelbyville Coca-Cola on Highway 53 south. It was one of only three Coca-Cola plants in the United States to operate without municipal sewers, hence the aerating lagoons in the background.

TRANSPORTATION

The Hempridge Depot, prior to 1900, included left to right, man on the horse is Waddy Thompson; the rider-less horse is the Jesse's "Old Parker;" Jim Martin; Claude Clark, depot clerk; first boy is George Jesse; second boy is Frank Jesse; third boy is Guthrie Jesse; fourth boy is Thomas Jesse Jr.; fifth boy is William Shepherd Jr.; the man in the door is Dr. William Shepherd; older man with beard is 90-year-old Lunsford Rucker; and the last man on the right is Millard Fillmore Jesse, station agent.

Engine No. 9 was a familiar sight working with The Shelby Railroad Company.

Hempridge was an important stop on the rail line. It had its own siding.

A horse barn in the background provides the framework for a surrey on the Ben Allen Thomas farm around the turn of the 20th century.

Lem Houston McCormack enjoys showing these McCormack House guests around Waddy. They are shown here in front of the depot.

John Shannon and Wanda Willett on carriage ride in about 1907.

Road building machines were busy paving Shelby County roads around 1910.

Prior to the coming of the auto in the early 1900s, Shelby County had many fine stables, including this one operated by Howard Harbison.

George Hanser and his sister Clara enjoy a buggy ride in August 1915.

Shannon Funeral Company hearses were drawn by horses in the early days.

The Southern Depot on south First Street was a very busy stopping place on the Southern Railway line.

Trestles enabled railroads to span creeks and rivers.

Another trestle permitted trains to cross Clear Creek and Brashears Creek.

Shelby County buggies and then cars were served by several covered bridges.

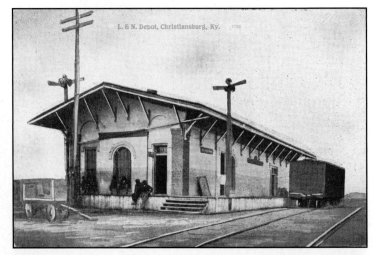

The L & N depot at Christiansburg was among the first in Shelby County.

Mighty steam engines were always a marvel to behold as they carried freight and passengers on the L & N and Southern main lines that served Shelbyville.

This picturesque scene shows the rail bed cut south of Finchville that had train service until 1935.

This Southern Railroad water tower was situated near Guist Creek.

One of the many traveling medical companies of the early 1900s is reflected in this J. R. Watkins rig and salesman.

The Interurban came to Shelbyville in 1912 and was the principal means of traveling from Shelbyville to Louisville. Many dairy farmers shipped their milk and other products to the Louisville market via the Interurban.

This is another view of the Interurban which is operating two passenger cars on this particular day.

The Waddy Depot was located on the main line of the Southern Railroad.

Water towers were essential to keeping the Interurban moving seven days a week.

Jane S. Heath drives John Shannon's car with young William L. Shannon and John Heath Jr. in the rumble seat.

William L. Shannon and dog "Pal" enjoy a ride in front of Shannon's Funeral Home at 8th and Main Streets.

The L & N station on north 8th Street had a very Victorian look in the early 1920s.

In 1926 Shelbyville's Coca-Cola plant was delivering bottles of Coca-Cola from this fleet of trucks which could carry 260 cases at a time.

George Bowles operated a "milk special" between Finchville and Louisville in the early 1930s.

Service on the Shelbyville-Finchville line had been discontinued when this photo was taken.

Blackie and Whitie Gray are anxious to get going on this tractor, but their father, Samuel Columbus Gray, is keeping a close eye on them. Whitie's given name is William Preston and Blackie's is Adriel Clark (after two prominent Shelby County physicians Dr. William Preston Hughes and Dr. Adriel Clark Weakley). An engineer, Samuel Gray helped convert the Climax Roller Mills from steam to diesel, and Our Best Mill in Smithfield from steam to electricity. Blackie and Whitie were three years old when their father died.

Reed Webb owned and operated the Webb Transfer Line in Shelbyville for many years. Tobacco was one of the principal commodities which it transported.

The Shelbyville airport enjoyed a brief period of popularity and activity after World War II, but by the 1950s there was practically nothing left to show that it had existed. Here, Bill Shannon, one of the early proponents of the airport, stands near an Aeronca airplane operated by Scharton Flying Service.

Reed Anderson, a very able impersonator of Groucho Marx, was trying to persuade the public to buy a Desoto, a Dodge-manufactured automobile that was discontinued in the 1940s.

Long and Weller made its name manufacturing and delivering concrete products.

Several dairies provided home delivery in Shelbyville for many years, including Bird's Dairy which was owned by Tate and Stuart Bird.

Terry Ethington and Susie Durrett have some fun in 1952.

The class of 1955 at Shelbyville High School prepares to embark on its senior trip to New York.

In a Civil War reenactment, "The General" came to town in 1962 at the L & N depot on north 8th Street.

This is a view of Shelbyville looking west from the bridge which brought travelers into town near 1st Street. The Glacier Ice Company may be observed on the left side, across the bridge.

This West Main Street home in the late 1800s belonged to Lyle Hocker and Sadie Hocker Walters.

Note the hitching post and arc lamp in this view of the fountain from the northeast corner of 5th & Main Streets at the turn of the 20th century.

This was how Shelbyville appeared from the observatory atop the old Shelby College on College Street.

This is an early view of Shelbyville as it appeared from high ground to the east of the city.

The old First Presbyterian Church was erected in 1846 and served the community until 1888 when it was replaced with a new building.

The First Baptist Church of Shelbyville was located on the southwest corner of 5th and Main Streets in 1860. It burned in 1909.

The former Centenary Methodist Church which stood on the corner of 5th and Main Streets.

The Church of the Annunciation (Catholic) was built in 1860.

The First Assembly Presbyterian Church, located on the southwest corner of 9th and Main Streets, was dedicated on Dec. 17, 1871. The property and lot on which the church was constructed was sold to J. M. Wakefield at public auction for $2650 in 1909. The building to the west of the church was the manse.

Allendale Farm was a county showplace in 1905.

The First Christian Church in the Italianate style was built at 4th and Main Streets in Shelbyville in the 1860s. It was destroyed by fire in 1969.

The Philip Weissinger family lived in this home on the Mt. Eden Road in 1905. Later, it became the Plantation Inn before it was demolished.

Around 1907 the Carriss family owned this house and farm on Pea Ridge Road. The boys in front are Gilbert, Cecil and Morton Carriss. Gilbert Carriss had two sons, F. B. and Wilmer who both farmed in Shelby County.

The John S. Shannon family lived in this East Main Street home.

W. P. Deiss, long-time Shelbyville book store owner, was born in this home on east Washington Street where the Stratton Community Center is currently located.

The St. John's Methodist Church was built in 1896 at a cost of $3,000.

The last Mulberry (Presbyterian) Church.

This building was known as the Tevis Cottage, after the famed administrators of Science Hill School. Dr. Kenny Gravett's office now stands where the cottage once stood.

The Episcopalians in Shelbyville trace their heritage back to 1856. It was in 1867 that their church at the corner of 3rd and Main Streets was completed. It was paid for in just four years.

The First Presbyterian Church as it appeared ion the 1940s.

The congregation of the Salem Baptist Church in 1895.

The Curtis P. Hall home on Magnolia Avenue in 1909.

The Philemon Bird home stood at the corner of 8th and Washington Streets. The property is now the location of a telephone company building

The Robert Giltner home in 1909.

This is Main Street facing west. Painted on horse-drawn delivery wagon is a Goodman Bros. & Co. sign. Goodman Bros, which later moved to Clay Street, was in business from 1903 to 1911 next to the courthouse.

The home of Col. Paul Bohn was located at 822 West Main Street. At one time it was the Elks Club.

The Tucker home on Ky. 147 at Clark Station.

A postcard denoting the Undulata Stock Farm.

The Robert A. Smith family lived in this home at 1124 Main Street. It is now the Shannon Funeral Home.

The J. C. Burnett family lived in this east Main Street home in 1910.

The John Ballard house, also known as the Winlock property, was located on the northeast corner of 3rd and Main Streets.

In 1910 Commander W. C. P. Muir built this home on the Old Taylorsville Road.

The John Fawkes home in the 700 block of north Main Street was located next to the current Shelbyville Welcome/Heritage Center.

The family of Samuel Monroe Long, founder of Climax Roller Mills, lived in this home at 1217 West Main Street.

Joshua Lee Payne and Lena Leona Johnson Payne built this house on the Mt. Eden Road. Their son, Louis Buckner Payne, is seen going in the front door. This house was later demolished to build a new home. Rocks from the old house formed the foundation for the new one.

L. G. "Pop" Smith, one of the co-founders of Smith-McKenney Drug Co., lived with his family in this home at 37 Main Street in 1910.

Attorney and Shelbyville Mayor Luther Willis and his family lived in this home at 1108 West Main Street in 1910.

George A. Armstrong built this home for his family in the early 1900s.

The Guthrie family home once stood at the end of Colony Drive, just off the Eminence Pike.

A band played during the Shelby County Fair at this ornate gazebo

The Fielding Ballard home stood at the intersection of Main and 11th Streets for many years. A service station and pizza store are located there in 2008.

Shelbyville's many warehouses spew smoke and soot during the wintertime.

This panoramic view taken at Main Street and Beechwood Avenue shows the Interurban tracks, the original Shell station, and the Sears-Roebuck home that is adjacent to the fairgrounds at Main Street and Smithfield Road.

The third building of the First Baptist Church is shown in a postcard. It was built in 1911 and collapsed in 1958 due to structural failure.

The Church of the Annunciation offered this interior view in 1955.

Parking meters dotted both sides of Main Street in this scene from 1970s downtown Shelbyville.

Another view of Main Street between 5th and 6th Streets.

A replica of the original blockhouse, which stood opposite the courthouse, was built in the early 1970s in preparation for the nation's bicentennial.

The "Shady Rest" (later called the Old Colonel) was a bus stop near Clayvillage in the 1930s.

The old Kings Daughters Hospital on Clay Street was built in 1906, with additions in 1907 and 1916.

The new Kings Daughters Hospital was finished in 1955.

The Amanda Smith Hospital for the Colored, later Daisy M. Saffell Hospital, opened in 1916.

Governor A. O. Stanley was born in this house on Washington Street in 1867. It became known as the Stanley-Casey Home and was owned and renovated by The Shelby County Historical Society beginning in 1995. It was sold to a group of attorneys in 2006.

The log home pictured here was moved to the corner of 7th and College Streets near Chatham Station.

Artie Mary Lee owned this pioneer log house which was located behind her home on Ashland Avenue.

"Artie Mary's" log cabin was furnished with authentic furniture, furnishings, guns, and other items from the nation's early years.

The building on the northwest side of 8th and Main Streets as it appeared when it was purchased by the Shelby County Community Theatre in 1979.

This is how the highly-acclaimed community theatre appears in 2008. The theatre's first show, "The Music Man," performed at Shelby County High School, was an outstanding success.

GOVERNMENT & POLITICS

A. O. Stanley was born in Shelbyville in a home on Washington Street in 1867. He served as Kentucky's governor from 1915 to 1919. This photo was taken in 1916.

The old jail at the corner of 5th and Main Streets. It was built in 1849.

Thomas S. Baxter was Shelbyville's first African-American council member. A Republican, he served from 1892 to 1910.

Work began on a new jail at the corner of 5th and Washinton Streets in 1891. This structure served the community until 1997 when a state-of-the-art facility opened on Snow Hill.

This was the first grand jury to convene, on Nov. 10, 1914, following the completion of the new courthouse at Fifth and Main Streets. From left to right in the top row are Sam Newton, George Mahuron, Charles Jennings, W. C. Buckman, Robert McDowell, Robert Sleadd, County Attorney Edwin Davis, and Commonwealth's Attorney Charles Sanford; seated are John Fawkes, James Price, James Wright, Mr. Green, Mr. Crawford, and John E. Brown.

Shelbyville gets its first fire truck in the early 1920s.

The fire department was located adjacent to the old Shelby County Trust building, now Commonwealth Bank & Trust Co.

The Shelbyville post office was headquartered in this building on 6th Street in 1910.

The Shelbyville Fire Department, located at the corner of 11th and Main Streets, was staffed in the 1960s by; front, Bill McClain, Corky Meeks, Eugene Bemiss, Eddie Smith, and Joe Best; back, Howard Flood, Bobby Likes, Charles Hatchett, Eugene White, Pete Wills, Ernest Hawkins, and E. J. Reed.

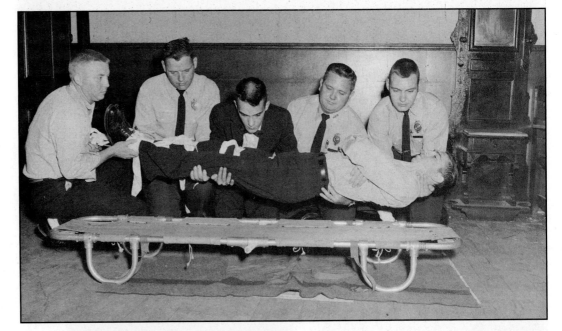

Another drill helped firemen stay attuned to possible emergencies.

The Fire Department stayed sharp by conducting various fire fighting and civil defense drills.

Still another drill showed firemen anxious to stay abreast of new techniques.

Officer Jake Brummett is seen in the late 1940s in front of Casey's store at 421 Main Street.

Work is well underway on Shelbyville's post office in 1927 at the corner of 7th and Main Streets.

The post office opened to the public in 1928. It was located on the site of the old Stuart's Female College.

This view of the post office was taken in the 1950s.

This is a side view of the old courthouse.

Shelby County's third courthouse was built between 1844 and 1845 and is shown here in 1910.

The old courthouse has been demolished in this view from 1912. Note that the fountain is still in the center of the street. It would be moved months later to accommodate the arrival of the Interurban.

Shelbyville's fourth courthouse is under construction in 1913.

A prayer is being offered as these men doff their hats at the dedication of the new courthouse.

Shelby County's fourth courthouse has served the county for nearly 100 years. Note the presence of many cars in the 1920s.

Louis Rothchild served as mayor of Shelbyville from 1912 to 1922. Other men who had served as mayor included John I. Logan (1894-1898), Luther C. Willis (1898-1906), Dr. T. E. Bland (1906-1910), and Lynn T. Gruber (1910-1912).

Curtis P. Hall was mayor from 1922 to 1930. He also started Hall & Son Lumber Co., later Hall & Davis.

Paul F. Schmidt served as mayor from 1930 to 1934.

Robert F. Matthews was the first person to be elected by the general public as mayor of Shelbyville. Previously, mayors had been elected by the city council. Matthews served as mayor from 1934 through 1945, and was succeeded by Lewis T. Frederick in January 1946. Unfortunately, declining health forced Mayor Frederick to resign three months into his term, and Matthews was selected by the council to serve out the remainder of his term. He was then re-elected in 1949.

Harold Y. Saunders succeeded Robert Matthews as mayor, serving from 1954 to 1958. Later, Saunders practiced law and then served as circuit judge from 1972 to 1992. When Saunders took office as mayor he received $50 per meeting; and councilmen earned $10 per meeting.. In 2008, Shelbyville's mayor receives $55,000 annually and council members $13,000.

Jesse Puckett served three terms as mayor, from 1958 to 1970. He then served as city clerk 15 years. Earlier, Puckett served one term as a city councilman.

Wyman Porter succeeded Jesse Puckett as mayor, serving without pay from 1970 to 1974.

Marshall Long succeeded Wyman Porter as mayor, serving from 1974 to 1982. Long became a successful state legislator, serving in both the House of Representatives and the State Senate.

This is a view of the old waterworks, just below Bunker Hill.

This is the old standpipe at Bunker Hill which held the city's entire water supply.

Mrs. Craig (Betsy) R. Schmidt, far left, was among those who greeted Mrs. Dwight D. Eisenhower when she came to Kentucky.

Alben Barkley was campaigning in 1954 for his old U. S. Senate seat when he came to Shelbyville. He had served as vice president under Harry S. Truman (1948-1952). Barkley died while making a speech at Washington & Lee University in 1956. Here he greets local Democratic chairman Howard Pearce, right, and Carol and Laban Jackson, left. Charlene Anderson Kresin peeks over Barkley's right shoulder.

Joe Biagi, left, introduced Senator John Sherman Cooper in 1954 during a U. S. Senate campaign stop in Shelbyville.

The Shelbyville City Council was sworn in on Jan. 3, 1955. Noteworthy was the appearance, far left, of Lee Nor Mack, first African-American elected since Thomas Baxter in 1892. Mack was a Democrat and Baxter a Republican. Others include, from the left, Joe Dedman, Sam Liss, Jeptha B. Tracy, Circuit Judge Coleman Wright, Mayor Jesse Puckett, Harry Long, and Sam Atlas.

A. B. "Happy" Chandler, one of two men to serve two separate terms as governor of the Commonwealth, came to Shelbyville in 1956 to help dedicate what was originally called Chandler Lake. Seated immediately behind him are Paul Ratcliff, Rev. J. Edward Cayce, and Jesse Puckett. The name of the lake was subsequently changed to Guist Creek Lake following the election of Bert Combs as governor.

Governor A. B. Chandler, far left, was on hand when Dr. B. F. Shields was honored on the occasion of his medical retirement in the late 1950s. Dr. Shields also served in Kentucky's House of Representatives in 1952-53, and in the State Senate 1954-57. Others include, left to right, Judge Coleman Wright, unidentified, Dr. Shields, Rev. J. Edward Cayce, Dr. Donald Chatham, and Lt. Gov. Harry Lee Waterfield.

This group of postal service employees gathered in the early 1960s. From left to right, are Alwyn Miller, Harold Stanley, Rodman Hansborough, Guy Lea, Bob Eggen, Benton Miller, and Jimmy Lapsley.

Governor Bert Combs, center, and State Finance Commissioner Robert Matthews Jr. were the principal speakers at the dedication of the new Shelby County High School. The trooper is Robert Howser, father of longtime Circuit Court Clerk Kathy Nichols. Matthews became the first and only Shelby Countian to serve as Attorney General, from 1963 to 1967.

Mary Louise Foust served three terms as state auditor for the Commonwealth of Kentucky and practiced law in Shelbyville and Lexington. She was the first woman in Kentucky to be both a licensed attorney and CPA. She ran unsuccessfully in 1963 to become Kentucky's first woman governor.

Bagdad natives Mae Hall Peniston and Wilma Yeary join Governor Wendell Ford as he signs a National Secretary's Week proclamation in April 1972.

W. Coleman Wright was judge of the 12th Circuit Court of Kentucky from 1952 until 1970.

Brig. Gen. R. R. Van Stockum, left, chairman of the Louisville Armed Forces Committee, introduces President Gerald R. Ford at the committee's 50th annual banquet. On the right is U. S. Representative Tim Lee Carter.

William E. Matthews is welcomed by U.S. President Jimmy Carter to the White House Conference on Rural Journalism in 1978. Matthews, who served as President of the Kentucky Press Association in 1977, represented the state's rural weekly and daily newspapers at the conference.

Shelby County benefited strongly from the longtime legislative service of attorney Louis T. Peniston, of New Castle, who represented Shelby County in the state legislature in 1964-67 and 1972-73. Altogether he served 25 years in the state legislature, 16 years in the House and 9 years in the Senate.

Bobby Stratton began serving the first of five terms as Shelby County Judge/Executive in 1978. Stratton, who had served eight years on the city school board, was also deeply involved in the city's Little League and sports programs for many years.

Several Shelby Countians were killed and others injured when a passenger train wrecked at Floyd's Fork Bridge on the Shelby-Jefferson County line in 1881.

Members of the G.A.R. (The Grand Army of the Republic) and their families gathered on Decoration Day at Grove Hill in 1887 to remember those who had fallen during the Civil War.

This group of Confederate men, women, and children remembered in 1887 their kinsmen and friends who had died in the Civil War.

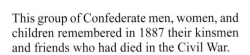

The family of J. Franklin Bell was honored by townspeople in 1902 following his triumphant return from service with the Philippine Expeditionary Force, 1898-1902. Here he appears in front of the George A. Armstrong home on West Main Street. Gen. Bell was born in Shelby County on Jan. 8, 1856 and died in 1919 after distinguishing himself in the Philippines and World War I. He is one of two Shelby Countians to be awarded the Congressional Medal of Honor. The other was awarded to Private John H. Callihan in 1861 during the Civil War.

The Shelbyville Fire Department was preparing to observe Decoration Day in 1904.

The ruins of the First Baptist Church following the fire that destroyed the church and several businesses in 1909.

These actors in a play at Mt. Eden in the early 1900s include left to right Henry G. Cleveland, Bill Kinder, Edgar Waters, Ruby Hardesty, Jim Hedden, Leola Harrison, Ottis Goodwin, Luella May, and O. H. Skyles.

The Knights of Pythias gathered at Tasso Lodge #14 on Feb. 15, 1915.

A May Day celebration at Shelbyville High School which opened in 1917.

Benefit Dance

For World's War Veterans' Hospital

Wednesday Evening, August 6, 1919

9:30 to 2:30 o'clock

Mammoth Rink, Shelbyville, Ky.

Smith's Saxaphone Sextette   Subscription $2.00

A dance to benefit World War I veterans was scheduled at the Mammoth Rink in 1919. Smith's saxophone sextet was to provide the music. Note the late hours of 9:30 to 2:30 a.m.

Your Are Invited to

Senior - Dedicatory Dance

Eminence High School's New Gym

Adm. $1.00 — Spectators 35c   10 til 2

FRIDAY, DECEMBER 4, 1936

—Featuring—

ANDY ANDERSON & HIS LADS

The University of Kentucky's 13 Piece Band of radio fame. Anderson is former Captain of U. K. Basketball team and former All-American.

—NO BREAKS—

1—
        "Sing, Baby, Sing"
2—
        "The Way You Look Tonight"
3—
        "My Dear"
4—
        "Star Dust"
5—
        "I Can't Escape From You"
6—
        "I Love You Truly"

MAY DANCE

Friday, May 8—Cropper Gym

—Music By—

LIEBER LAGER

—NO BREAKS—

1—
        'Lost"
2—
        "Beautiful Lady in Blue"
3—
        "What's the Name of That Song"
4—
        "It's Been So Long"
5—
        "Lights Out"
6—
        "Sophisticated Lady"
1st Extra—
        "St. Louis Blues"
2nd Extra—
        "Dinner For One, Please James"
HOURS—10 to 2   ADM. Couple $1.00
        Stags 75c

Shelby County youngsters were invited to attend the dedication of Eminence High School's new gym on Dec. 4, 1936. Music was being provided by the University of Kentucky's Andy Anderson's 13-piece band of "radio fame."

Admission was only $1.00 for couples and 75 cents for "stags" when Lieber Lager provided the music for a dance at the Cropper Gym.

"Water, water everywhere" covered "Mrs. Roemmele's bottom" just north of Jail Hill bridge. Mrs. Roemmele was Paul Bohn's grandmother.

On Feb. 1, 1937, Funeral Director Ralph Catlett gave Mrs. Augusta Carriss a receipt for $315 in full payment for services rendered upon the death of J. H. Carriss.

E. J. Cline was president and T. R. Webber secretary when the Shelby County A & M Association issued this Shelby County Fair coupon book in 1940.

The front cover of the horse show program at the 1946 Shelby County Fair featured the likeness of "Noble Kalarama." The horse was standing at View Point Farm, owned by B. P. Eddie & Son. Lester Gibbs was president and Phillip Moesser secretary of the fair association.

The infield was the place to see and be seen in the 1940s at the Shelby County Fair. The Shelbyville High School band, located under the gazebo, played in the afternoons and evenings.

Lawson's Department Store ran a full-page ad, "Are We Thankful?" in The Shelby Sentinel extolling the greatness of Shelby County.

In 1948 several hundred people, including many school children, awaited the arrival of President Harry S. Truman's train that was carrying him across America in his memorable "Whistle Stop Tour."

These "Girls in Action" were coronated at the First Baptist Church in 1952.

Firemen battle a blaze at the Standard Garage on Washington Street.

Another blaze brings out firemen to battle flames and smoke at 6th & Clay Streets.

The Cropper School burned in the 1950s.

Firemen were summoned to the Shelby Office Equipment Co. where a fire broke out on the second floor.

Heavy rains generally produced flood-like conditions at the intersection of 8th & Main Streets for many years.

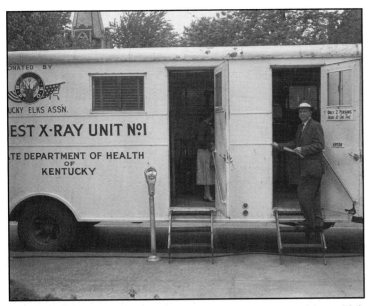

Mayor Harold Saunders checks out the chest x-ray machine which was located in front of the courthouse.

This group of young ladies is lining up for a chest x-ray in the 1950s.

THE FIRST BAPTIST CHURCH
Shelbyville, Ky.   April 19, 1959

ONE YEAR AGO

OUR CHURCH IN RUINS

OUR CONGREGATION STUNNED

OUR FUTURE UNCERTAIN

OUR PLANS INCOMPLETE

The ceiling of the First Baptist Church collapsed in 1958. Organist Mrs. B. B. Bailey had just left the building where she had finished practicing on the organ in preparation for Sunday services.

Judge Ada Carter begins the arduous task of picking the winners in the annual baby contest at the Shelby County Fair.

The Bookmobile representing free library service was an immensely popular attraction as it traveled about the county in the 1950s and 60s.

Everett Hall, right, helps with the ribbon presentation at the Shelby County Fair.

A crowd was on hand when the WHAS brought its Kentucky Barn Dance Show to the fairgrounds.

Randy Atcher and "Cactus" Tom Brooks were popular headliners with The Old Kentucky Barn Dance. Here, they played before an overflow crowd at the Shelby County Fairgrounds.

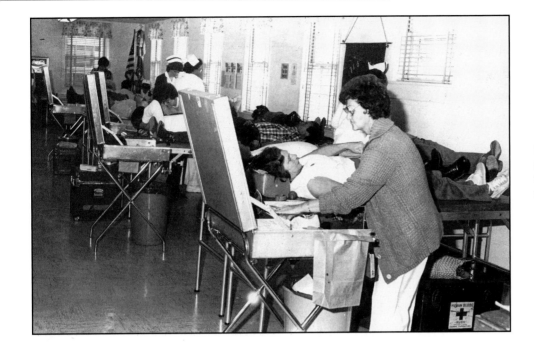

Shelby Countians understood the importance of giving blood during the drives which were held several times a year. This drive was held at the Centenary Church.

County Judge Ralph Mitchell speaks at the dedication of the new Kings Daughters Hospital in 1953. Mayor Robert Matthews in on the far right.

The Catholic Lawn Fete at the Church of the Annunciation was a popular attraction during the summer.

Elephants parading down Main Street signaled the coming of the circus. Such events were sometimes held on Snow Hill and at other times at the fairgrounds. Notice that traffic is still two-way.

Saturday nights were still big at and around the Shelby Theatre in 1960.

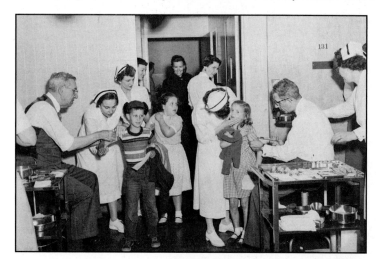

White youngsters line up for their polio shots in the early 1960s. Dr. Livingston Wahl and Dr. A. C. Weakley are administering the injections.

African-American youths get their injections from Red Cross nurses.

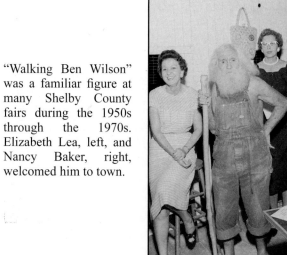

"Walking Ben Wilson" was a familiar figure at many Shelby County fairs during the 1950s through the 1970s. Elizabeth Lea, left, and Nancy Baker, right, welcomed him to town.

The threat of nuclear war had some Shelby residents building their own bomb shelters. Here, Katherine Cleveland and son Jim examine a shelter out in the county.

These youngsters were enjoying a 4th of July parade in the early 1960s. From left to right are Ben Mills, Pam Mills, Rhonda Miller, Cindy Tygrett, Louise Atwood, Bill Mills, Debbie Tygrett, Jim Cleveland, and Eddie Adams.

The Shelbyville Rotary Club has been taking up tickets at the Shelby County Fair for many years. From left to right are Roy Miller, Bill Scearce, Briggs Lawson, Ralph Mitchell, Roy Ratcliff, John Stout, Ted Hall, and Jim Leeds.

Trotters at the Shelby County Fair "rack on."

It would be hard to determine "who's the fairest of them all" in this grouping of lovely young ladies at the Shelby County Fair.

Pitchpipe and program from the Burley Tones.

The singing Burley Tones included front row, left to right: Bob Ballard, Sid Wilson, Bill King, Benton Miller, Al Miller, Director Paul Husband, Russell Hickman, Jimmie Stammerman, Bob Whitney, Paul Johnson, and Dean Ellis.; second row, left to right: Ernest Lyons, Joe Wise, Danny Wilson, Rebel Swigert, Dr. Rodney Whittaker, Jimmie Adams, Benny Lanter, Earl Sorrells, Jr., Guy Lea, Johnny Mathis, and Woody Mitchell. Third row, left to right: Paul LeCompte, Larry Ellis, Dr. K. E. Ellis, Bob Singleton, Ted Igleheart, Melvin Sams, Billy Connell, and Jack Roberts.

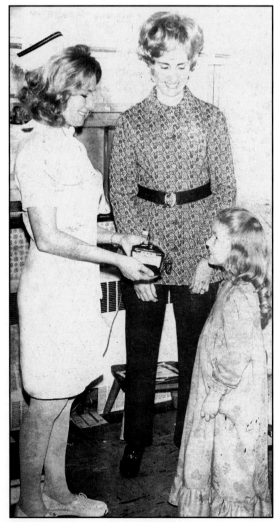

Charlotte Bond and her daughter Laurie, along with registered nurse Mrs. John Sharpe Jr., pose for an advertisement for an upcoming blood drive.

Shelbyville High School teacher Caroline Goodson will be remembered for her "Latin banquets" during the 1960s and 70s. In the background are Sue Carol Streable, Charles Long, Paul Schmidt, and Logan Brown.

The station "on the move" was built in 1870.

In 1971 Dr. Don Chatham dons his engineer's cap as he assists in moving the old L & N station from its longtime location on north 8th Street to a new location on north 7th Street. The building is still known as Chatham Station in honor of the family that helped preserve this historic building.

James Clark is on the scene at the site of a Southern Railway derailment in the 1970s.

The Centenary United Methodist Church was destroyed by fire in 1978.

Harry Mitchell is remembered for his many years of playing the organ at the Shelby County Fair.

The First Baptist Church Life Singers in 1977 included front row, Rick Magallon, Co-Director, patrons Richard Ellis, Ethel Martin, Marion Boyd, Mark and Peytie Scearce, Dr. Don Chatham, Founder and Co-Director Betty Jean Chatham, Colonel and Mrs. Harland Sanders, Mr. and Mrs. H. B. Kinsolving, and Mr. and Mrs. Morris Adams.

AGRICULTURE, TOBACCO AND THE FESTIVAL

Joseph Albert Lawrence stands in front of a large mule barn on the Benson Pike.

J. F. Middleton was known for his Maple Grove Jersey cows. "Derry's Rosa" is on display here in 1909.

In 1910 William H. Giltner owned this large stock barn.

The largest stock barn in Kentucky belonged to Phillip Weissinger. It's now the clubhouse and storage barn for Weissinger Hills Golf Course.

These fine Jersey cattle from Allen Dale farm were on display in 1915.

The George E. Hanser clan (he is sitting on the fender of the tractor) was hard at work in 1917. His brothers and sisters were there to help.

President Ben Allen Thomas II signed these 17 shares of Western District Warehousing Corporation stock ($1.00 par value) in June 1927.

The Rotary and Kiwanis Clubs joined to welcome farmers to the annual Farm-City Banquet in 1957. In later years only the Kiwanis Club continued the tradition.

Robert Tyler Long steers the tractor while David Long enjoys riding on the Long Silo & Block float in the Tobacco Festival of the early 1950s.

Republican Governor Simeon Willis obviously enjoys his "work" of crowning Charles Abrams Jr. of Mt. Eden and Evelyn Bryant of Cropper as the King and Queen at the annual Tobacco Festival in 1947.

Gilbert Carriss, Dora Carriss, Wilmer Carriss, Arley Franklin and Leora Franklin weed tobacco on the J. B. Cook farm in 1962.

A life-extending invention, this iron lung was displayed at the Tobacco Festival by the Shelby County Chapter of the March of Dimes.

Two airplanes "fly over" the Tobacco Festival parade. Note the Goodyear store located in the 600 block of Main Street.

Mary E. Pfost and Billy Andriot Jr. were the Tobacco Festival prince and princess at the Shelbyville Elementary School.

Clarence Proctor, shown here with his prize roadster, operated Proctor Paving Company for many years in partnership with his brother Bob.

These cheerleaders from Mt. Eden travel past Pearce Motor Company, which at that time was located at the corner of 4th & Main Streets.

"Doc" Headen's Service Station on the south side of Main Street between 7th and 8th Streets offered this float. Note the telephone number: 42.

Nancy Bottom and Paul Robert (Bud) Hall represented Cropper in the Tobacco Festival in the mid-1950s.

The City Café was a popular eating establishment on the north side of Main Street between 7th and 8th Streets. Those seated on the float are left to right: Tennie Cubert, Jenny Wallace, Agnes Rayland, Belle Swanson, and Colline Jennings.

The Thunderbird was a sensation when it was introduced by the Ford Motor Company. Here it graces the Pearce Motor Co. float.

McGinnis Transfer Line and Western Auto shared this float.

These princes and princesses enjoyed riding on the Mark J. Scearce float in 1952.

Future Governor Martha Layne Hall (later Collins) was the 1954 Burley Tobacco Festival Queen. She is on the far left.

Main Street swarmed with citizens of the city and county at each Tobacco Festival.

In 1957 Andriot's Men's Shop and Mary's Frock Shop shared this float in the big parade. Billy Andriot and Janet Garner are in the rear of the float, while Nancy and Jane Shannon are seated at the front.

The Shelbyville High School Band steps out smartly at the head of the annual Shelby County Tobacco Festival Parade in the 1940s. A sign for Blakemore's Grocery may be spotted on the right hand side of the photo. Blakemore's began doing business in downtown Shelbyville in the 1920s. Other signs advertise Admiral radios, and Bill's Auto Parts.

The coon dog race was always a popular feature of each Tobacco Festival. Here the dogs cross the finish line near the old Shelby Co. Trust Bank (now Commonwealth Bank & Trust).

Ruben's Dry Goods, which was located next to the Farmers & Traders Bank, was a downtown mainstay for many years.

These pretty lasses adorned the float of Bowles-Martin, which used the slogan "Say It with Flowers."

This majestic float carried Carol Lou Barlow Smith, Sue Bradbury, and Ann Maupin, with Julia Hopkins in the rear.

The Statue of Liberty was displayed by a local Boy Scout unit.

Martha Layne Hall (later Collins) with the new King and Queen of the Tobacco Festival, Sam West and Ginny Wright.

The crowds were everywhere on Tobacco Festival Day, including these folks sitting atop the buildings on the north side of the street between 6th & 7th Streets.

Queen candidates in the early 1960s included Sue Marshall, Bonnie Burks, unidentified, Vickie Wilhoite, Suzanne Amyx, and Joy Hopkins.

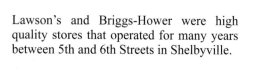

Lawson's and Briggs-Hower were high quality stores that operated for many years between 5th and 6th Streets in Shelbyville.

Dr. and Mrs. Wiley T. Poynter were in charge of Science Hill School in 1889 The school opened in 1825 and operated successfully for 114 years before closing in 1939. During that time it had only six individuals who helped oversee the instruction and training, including Julia Ann and John Tevis (1825-1870), Dr. Wiley T. Poynter (1870-1896), and Clara, Harriett and Juliet Poynter (1896-1939)

The Poynters with their faculty and students in 1892.

Stuart College attracted these passers-by and students in the 1890s; Pattie Burton, Bettie Blanton, John P. Allen, Prof. Winchester Hall Stuart, Pete North, Miss Arnold, Mrs. S. M. Long, and Mr. Courtney.

Shelby College was located on College Street. Note the observatory atop the building. It was from this observatory that a full eclipse of the sun was observed in 1869.

The observatory is missing in this later photo of Shelby College.

Thomas Doolan's School, aka Shelby Academy, was located at Finchville in 1890.

Students at Clayvillage Academy in 1899 included, front row, left to right, Laura "Lollie" Vannatta, Beulah Newton; unidentified, Stella Brooks, Grace Clark, unidentified, Susie Serber, Charles Grant Jones, Owen Sleadd, Ollie Clark, unidentified; middle row, left to right, George Kent, unidentified, Mattie Lee Vannatta, Earl Clark, Elmer Serber, Lynn Serber; back row, Will Davis, Harry Serber, unidentified, Grovener Snook, unidentified teacher, Ben Davis, and Marshall "Toad" Clark.

The fourth grades at Science Hill in 1930 included back row, Mary Ann Biagi, Marcella Donahue, Mary Brainard Bell, Frances Dale, Catherine Smith, Teacher Miss VanArsdel, Joan Castleman, Anna Lee Hardesty, Catherine Owen, and Sam Castleman; second row, Anna Louise Caudill, Betsy Hanna, Frances Stone, Betsy Mason Stanley, Winona Allen; seated, Christine Arvis Ray, Lilly Wallace, A. C. Weakley, Beverly Logan, Lucille Hart, Lloyd Jones, and Day Allen Cassiday.

The faculty and students shown here are at the Finchville school in 1909.

Susan Fawkes is the well dressed lady in this early 1900s photo beside the city library.

This is the original Mulberry School on the Cropper Road. The teachers lived at the Ben Allen Thomas farm located across the road. Ben Allen Thomas II and Vestina Belle Bailey, who were later married, met at the school when they were children.

Shulkeys School of Telegraphy was located near Main and 1st Streets.

These students attended the Ashland two-room school.

The Ashland School was located on the Benson Pike in 1926.

Professor E. J. Paxton and the faculty of Central Normal College operated the school at Waddy for a number of years around the turn of the century.

Central Normal College was located on this site. When it went out of business in the early 1900s it was turned into the Waddy School.

The original Waddy elementary and high school was built in 1914. It was replaced by a brick structure when it was destroyed by fire in 1916.

Teachers who taught at Waddy in 1938 included left to right and married names, Blanche Melear Hansen, Verna Lawson Headen, Billie Van Arsdale, Kitty Martin Garrett, and Nellie Cox Richards.

W. R. (Roy) Martin served as principal, coach, and teacher at the Waddy school for many years. This photo was taken in 1965 when he was 70 years of age.

The Waddy senior class of 1946 included left to right, Billy Hornback, Jake Ritter, Kathrine Murphy, Coleman Burk, and Waddy Jesse.

Berea Hall at Lincoln Institute was built in 1911 in the Collegiate Gothic Style.

Mrs. Bessie Overstreet was the teacher of these youngsters who attended Clark Station Elementary School.

The children of Rev. Charles Davis are included in this group from the Old Montclair Elementary School.

Lincoln Institute graduated this group of young men and women in 1930.

Marnel C. Moorman, Shelby Country educator, was the first African-American vice president and president of the Kentucky Education Association, serving several terms in both positions.

These youngsters were playing at the High Street School in Martinsville prior to the end of segregation.

Teachers at the Finchville School educated hundreds of students between 1915 and 1976 when it closed. It was later razed.

The students on the left from High Street elementary school are not identified. The teachers include left to right, Mrs. E. Byrd, Mrs. D. Dale, Mrs. R. Radcliffe, Mrs. J. Dale, Mrs. V. Purdy, Mrs. Taylor, Mr. Marnell Moorman, Mrs. M. Brown, Mrs. F. Stone, Mrs. W. Mathis, and Mrs. Thomas.

At one time Mt. Eden educated students from the first through the senior grades. The high school closed in 1950 and students began going to Waddy High. Elementary and junior high students continued their schooling in Mt. Eden until the school closed in the early 1960s.

Elementary and Junior High teachers at Mt. Eden in 1958-59 included, first row, Frances Catlett, Ora Nethery, Minnie Sue Nethery, and Minnie Nethery; second row, Lois Martin, Elizabeth Cook, Mrs. Baker and Frances Shelburne.

Teachers at the Finchville School included Miss Tackett (math) and Miss Mary Elizabeth Lewis (history).

Second grade students at Mt. Eden School included front row, Barbara Figg, Mary Ann Collins, Martha Sparrow, Roxanne Travis, Barbara Gordon, and Susan Nethery; second row, Lonnie Cook, Vivian Carriss, Cathy McLain, Bill Newton, Cynthia Nation, Ronnie Webb, and Ricky Perry; third row, Jerry Simpson, Keith Ruble, unidentified, Keith Hall, Dale Jefferies, Gil Lawson, and Carol Murphy; fourth row, Terry Ingram, Vickie Barr and Junior Cook. The teacher is Miss Stratton.

The 8th grade class at Simpsonville in 1951 included front row, left to right, Buddy Rutledge, Horace McMullan, Rita Roby, Ruth Mae Connor, Sue Robinson, Lorine Parker, Tommy Lou Rudy, and Larry Miller; second row, Miss Marian Cardwell, Fulton Cottrell, Louis Rankin, Hobie Henninger, unidentified, unidentified, Alline Kinder, Judy McClain, and Ralph Bradford; third row, Randy Williams, Laura Estes, Shirley Hedges, C. T. Phillips, and Billy Doyle; fourth row, Manzy Lyles, unidentified, Pauline Kinder, Bonnie Shelbourne, Charles Druin, Marshall Blevin, and Calvin Tipton.

Joe Beach, left, appears here with the Simpsonville band which was the beginning of what would become the Shelby County band.

The Simpsonville Class of 1957 gets ready to board the C & O in Shelbyville for the senior trip.

A packed house enjoyed a school performance at the Simpsonville gym.

The Shelbyville library was one of many beneficiaries of millionaire Andrew Carnegie who provided funding for hundreds of public libraries across the country.

Longtime librarian Catherine Nicholas checks out a book to one of the many youngsters who patronized the local library.

Prof. H. V. Tempel, far left, and Mrs. Tempel, far right, dedicated many years to the students of Henry Clay High School in the eastern end of the county. This is a class in 1955.

Parents and friends of Shelby County High School students enjoyed a concert in the school's auditorium.

These youngsters were students at Shelbyville Graded School between 1915 and 1917. In the front are Ben Arrington, G. Davis, M. Wimp, V. Bell, J. Roberts, Bernard Davis, and Paul Hardesty; rear, T. Roberts, H. A. (Gus) Barnett, Miss Pope, Jimmy Burnett, and Henry Bodkin.

The sophomore class at Shelbyville High School in 1909 included left to right, front row, Bernard Bailey, Merritt James, Lewis Gruber, Theodore Band; second row, Virginia Boyd, Robert Brow, Julia Dale, J. J. Byars, Bessie Fawkes, L. D. Zaring; top row, Sylvia Sanders, Robert Smith, Della Heilman, Edwin Coots, Lucille Vannatta, Carl Smith, and Elizabeth Hansbrough.

Shelbyville High School was completed in 1917.

In 1929 Shelbyville High School students wore caps and gowns for the first time. In the front are Mary Harriet Caldwell, William McMakin, Cornell Jesse, Froman Ratcliffe, Mary Goodman, James Burnett, Roberta Cowherd, and John Kirk; back, Grace Butler, David Foust, Pauline Doyle, Hoskins Nichols, Florence Puckett, Ruth Willis, George Hill and Zenomia McDade.

Shelbyville 7th grade students in 1933 included, front row, H. B. Kinsolving, Neville Mahoney, King Walters, Robert Newton, Frank Calvin, Chester Brown, Don Richie, and Jesse Maddox; second row, John Guthrie, Brien Risk, Billy Garrett, William Ellwanger, Harold Stanley, George Happel, Craig Schmidt, Mrs. Sullivan (teacher); third row, Raymond Tinsley, Mary Ruth Yates, Charlotte Pryor, Julia Scruggs, Karen Abraham, Gladys Jones, and Mary Elizabeth Brown; fourth row, W. T. Conn, Louise Turner, Della Cinnamon, Juanita Bohan, Hallie Sharp, Pauline Diem, Fredrica Miller, Lois Hatchet and Gladys Mae Cline. (Jesse Maddox and Robert Newton were killed in World War II.)

The Shelbyville High Student Council in 1937 was composed of Mr. Hankins and Miss Lewis as advisors. Officers were President, George Robinson; Vice-President, Bill Shannon; Secretary, Betsy Hanna; and Treasurer, Lillian Huss. Additional members were Peytie Ballard, Billy Chenault, Gilbert Ellis, Jessie Floyd, Sue Fullenwider, Eddie Hall, Virginia Hanna, Harvey Hanser, Vivian Harp, Anna Lee Hardesty, Johnny Milton, Ruth Porter, Julia Lee Scruggs, Ed Stratton, Ben Allen Thomas, Herman Whitaker, and Craig Schmidt.

Mrs. B. B. Bailey taught English at Shelbyville High School for many years. She was also an organist at the First Baptist Church.

The "Tri-High Circle" at Shelbyville High School in 1946 included George Willis III, Howard Logan, Quentin Biagi, Katherine Barnett, Mary C. Briscoe, and Margaret Aldridge.

The Shelbyville High School band in 1947-48 was directed by Joe Beach.

Mrs. Willie C. Ray served as superintendent of schools from 1930 to 1960.

The 1953 Tri-Hi Circle top six students include front, left to right, Nancy Newton, Julia Stapleton, and Ann Turner Jennings; top, left to right, Fred Bond, Charles Mischler, and Achille Biagi.

Bruce Daniel was principal at Shelbyville High School for 20 years, from 1934 to 1954 and ended his teaching career at Eastern High School in Jefferson County. He was a five-letter athlete at Georgetown College and a highly successful Red Devils football coach from 1928 to 1946. His teams won 82 games, lost 43, and tied 5.

The 1951 Tri-Hi Circle members are center, front, Betty Ann Fawkes; back, left to right, Bob Hubbard, Jean Turner, Joe Cleveland, Sara Jane Blakemore, and Homer Petrou.

Drill team members; Sue Marshall, Martha Guthrie Flood, Judy Thacker, Suzanne Amyx, Patty Crawford, and Estelle Griffen.

These performers brought Jane Austen's "Pride and Prejudice" to life in 1966 at Shelbyville High School. In the back row are; Doug Potter, H. B. "Benton" Kinsolving IV, Don Chatham, Hunter Moody, and Thomas Lynn Richie; front, Charlene Chatham, Loretta Moore, Libby Schmidt, Alice Amyx, Sharon Kemper, and Bibby McKay.

Caroline Goodson, lower left, with her Latin Club at Shelbyville High School.

193

The 1967 kindergarten class of Mrs. Edmund (Mary David) Myles included front row, John Shannon, Mark Cowherd, Mark Stivers, Todd Brown; middle row, Stacey Nichols, Diane Davis, Laura Lee Goodman, Susan Hayes, Janice Yount, Sue Lou Hower, Mary Dan Easley, Jennifer Purnell, Mary Lee Mattingly, Beth Kimbrough; back row, Mrs. Kenneth Yount, Mrs. Casper Hayes Jr., Mrs. Joe Mattingly, Mrs. William Borders, Mrs. Horace Brown, and Mrs. Myles.

Mrs. Myles' 1974 kindergarten group included front row, Cynthia Griffith, Alan Zaring, Cliff Davis, Stephen Leonard, Bland Matthews, and John Massey; middle row, Jacqueline Simpson, John Robert Coots, Ricky Meadows, Susan McMullan; back row, Mrs. Myles, Daphne Sutherland, Angela Poulter, John Lawson, Chip Reed, John Robert Coots, and David Ethington.

Mrs. Myles' 1979 class included front row, Benny Evans, Todd Broughton, Sam Taylor, Shane Nethery; middle row, Ann Wilson Mathis, Missy Schmidt, Marsha Case, and Kate Bemiss; back row, Melissa Houser, Apryl Floyd, Meg Wilson, Jane Garrett, and Dana Nethery.

McClarty Hundley's 1964 kindergarten class included back row, Teresa Borders, Molly Craig, Steven Thomas, Susan Lawson, Rhonda Miller, and Julia Buckner; middle row, Scott Porter, Terri Long, David Logsden, Blythe Collings, David Harris, Mary Shannon, Carla Graybeal, Lena Easley, and Robin Nichols; front row, Harry Bird Hundley, Billy Hisle, J. Charles Kresin, Ben Fay, Ross Webb, Ward Wilson, and Teddy Igleheart.

Mr. and Mrs. John Kalmey and their twins, Janet and Joyce, attend a book fair at Southside Elementary School.

These youngsters put on a school play at Northside Elementary School in 1960. They included left to right, Sandy Scearce, John Hall, Sharon Kemper, Deborah Lawrence, Hunter Moody, Jerry Adams, and Doug Potter.

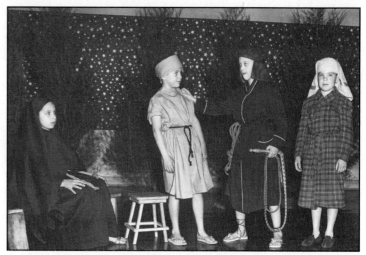

A large crowd enjoyed a May Day celebration at Northside Elementary School in the 1940s.

A Christmas play at Northside Elementary School featured Teresa Burge, Dennis Bailey, Jonnie Wigginton, and Todd Davis.

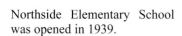

Northside Elementary School was opened in 1939.

Mothers pick up their first graders after their first day of school at Northside Elementary School in 1952.

Northside Elementary School 1952 1st grade students included front, left to right: Miss Marshall, Danny Jackson, Bobby Nickleson, Emma Searcy, Billy Bridge, Barry Warren, Linda Ingram, Garnett Gardner, Rusty Guthrie, Linda Aldridge, Carol Nichols, Jimmy Harrod, Joan Culver; second row, left to right: Patsy Jane Mathews, Connie Mackey, Alice Faye Williams, James Lee, Sally Smoot, Clay Powell, Randy Ballard, John Cleveland, Pat Rodgers, Bridwell Terhune, Judy Sacra, Barbara Wilson, Jennie Dean Barrickman, Bonnie Riddell; back row, left to right: Neil McClain, Kenneth Drane, Connnie Shouse, Scotty Gillock, Jerry Tracy, Freda Bustle, and Billy Anderson.

Plays were always popular at Southside Elementary School. Holding frame from left are Janet Thompson and Elaine Wilborn.

These "Cowboys and Indians" in the living picture at Southside Elementary School included clockwise from the mid-left, Dale Davis, Ricky Meadows, Johanna Smith, Curtis Hardesty, and Robert Tingle.

In 1967 this group of 8th graders at Shelbyville Junior High School, provided ground control for astronauts Linzie Craig, Ricky Burgin and Doug Logan as they set a three-day record inside the pictured space capsule, a record that held for four years.

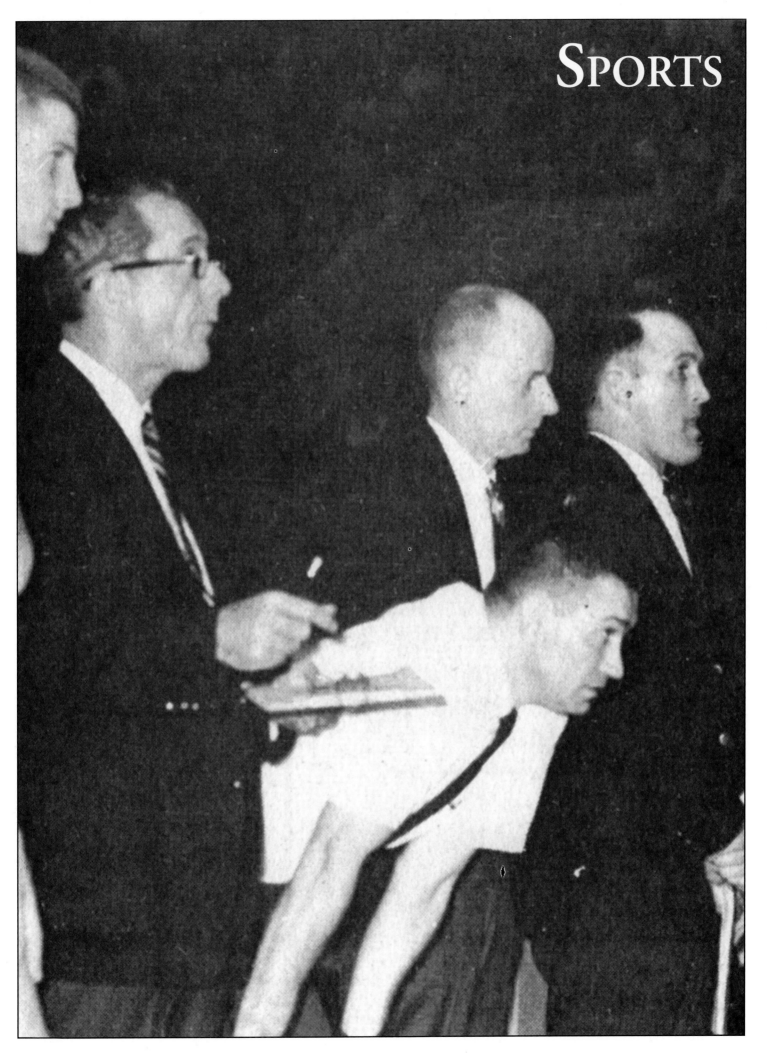

SPORTS

Dan McGann

The McGann brothers, Dan and Dennis, present historians with a puzzle. Dead ball era first baseman Dan "Cap" McGann's grave at Grove Hill Cemetery is on the right in this view. He was born in Shelbyville in 1871, and is the only Shelby County native to play in baseball's World Series, captaining the New York Giants in the 1905 classic. Dan was an uncle to Daniel and James "Buddy" O'Sullivan who owned and operated The Shelby Sentinel for many years. In his big league career, McGann batted .285 while playing for five different teams. He broke in with Boston in 1896, then played for Baltimore and St. Louis before joining the Giants from 1903 to 1907. He finished with Boston in 1908. He died in Louisville in 1910 at the age of 39.

This team that represented Shelbyville in the early 1900s. Games were played at the old Coots Park, at the north end of 2nd Street where Little League games were played in the 1970s.

This is the Shelbyville team that represented the locals in the old Bluegrass League. Hall of Famer Casey Stengel made his professional debut in Shelbyville in 1910 as a member of the Maysville team. Maysville edged Shelbyville by one run and a near riot ensued because of Stengel's shenanigans. Police had to escort the Maysville team out of town.

Longtime Shelbyville School Superintendent Mrs. Willie C. Ray coached this local championship team which included, left to right, Mrs. Lindsey Logan, Mrs. Charlton P. Nash, Mrs. Bernice Ellwanger Bond, Beulah Woolbright, Mrs. Oliver H. Raymond, and Nell Wilson Sweeney.

The Cropper High School team in 1919 included left to right, Thelma Hundley Roberts, unidentified, Ethel Hall Shaw, Stella Davis, Coach North, Corine Davis, and Irene Brown.

These young ladies were playing tennis on the court behind Science Hill School in the early 1900s.

The Gleneyrie High School team in 1941-42 included left to right, cheerleaders Margaret Hall (Ellis), Charlotte Graybill (Hall), and Louise Collins (Satterly); front row, Joe Carter, Walter Ruh, Harold Rogers, Russell Jackson, Wally Frazier, and Buddy Rogers; back row, Herman Moore, E. M. Jones, Gilbert Casey, Gilbert Ruble, Bob Giltner and coach Harry Lancaster.

The Mt. Eden High School team in the 1940s included left to right, back row, Kenneth Eggen, Charles Abrams Jr., L. W. Shields, James Carriss, and Eddie Cleveland; second row, Jess Martin Jr., Paul Glass, Steven Collins; front row, Bobbie Shouse, George Stucker, and Billy Shouse.

Another Mt. Eden High School team from that era included, left to right, Ray Lisby, Phil Hardesty, Billy Shouse, Charles Abrams Jr., Kenneth Crump, L. W. Shields, A. J. Martin Jr. John Glass Jr., John T. Butts, and James Carriss.

This cheerleading squad contained Stella Phillips, Patty Nethery, Marjorie Bemiss, and Peggy Hardesty.

Mt. Eden High School teams were coached by Walter Burk and Morris Chilton.

The Waddy High School baseball team in 1907 included back row, Harmon Nash (later a prominent Shelby County physician), Lem H. McCormack, Henry Young, Claude Frye, Selbert Proctor, and Thurston Waddy; front row, Guy Morton, Estes Snider, Arthur Secrest, and Jim McClain. The batboy was Kenneth (no last name provided).

The Waddy High School girls' basketball team of 1922 included front row, Elizabeth Dunnigan, Matt Norton; back row, Eleanor Robertson, Olivia Elliott, Katherine Robertson, Mary E. Hedden, and Georgia Elliott.

The Waddy High School girls basketball team of 1923 included left to right, W. R. (Roy) Martin, principal and coach, Mary Evelyn Hedden, Katherine Robertson, Matt Lula Norton, Blanche Melear, Eleanor Robertson, Lillian "Dick" Hedden, Olivia Elliott, and Georgia Elliott.

The Waddy High School basketball team of 1923 included left, to right, Coach Martin, George McCampbell, Stanley Hanks, Jessie Lacefield, Arch Thomas "Mutt" Dunnigan, Otto Norton, Robertson Rodmen, and John F. Martin.

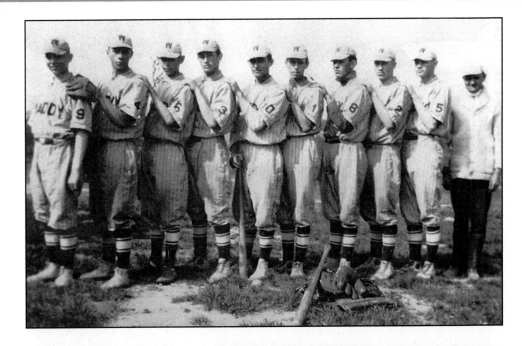

The Waddy High School baseball team of 1926 included left to right, John Martin, Roscoe Carpenter, Lewellyn Bohannon, Arch Thomas Dunnigan, Otto Norton, Jesse Lacefield, Stanley Hankins, Richard Milton, George J. McCampbell, and Coach Martin.

The Waddy High School basketball team of 1935-36 included back row, Kenneth Lisby, Bill Elder, Hollie B. Cheak; front row, Robert Wilson, Lem McCormack, Carl Shouse, and Virgil Cowherd.

The Waddy High School team of 1945-46 included front row, Billy Kenneth Gordon, Ralph Burk, Ralph Hatchell, Raymond Jesse, and Jake Ritter; back row, Coach Joe Donovan, Manager Lee Stratton, Billy Hornback, Coleman Burke, John Will Casey, and Manager Waddy Jesse.

The Waddy High School basketball team of 1948-49 included front row, Maurice Sea, Duvall Burk, Ralph Cook, Carroll Blackaby, Kenneth Cook, Roscoe Truman, and Gene Gaines; back row, Donnie Ritter, Bobby Watts, Otha Garrett, Garnett Moffett, Principal Roy Martin, Bobby Wells, John Will Casey, Jackie Meeks, and J. R. Bradley.

Several players from Shouse's Grocery (Waddy) fast pitch softball team in 1951 included left to right, Bobby Neal, Gary Ritter, Bobby Spencer, Junie Shouse and Doug Witt.

These Waddy Warriors won the Sinai Western Basketball Tournament in Anderson County in 1957. The front row includes; Eddie Raisor, Marin Reynolds, Ralph Sharp, Ray Gardner, Bobby Spencer, Bobby Casey, Johnny Miller, Will Logan Clark, Charles McCormack, and Ronnie Tindall; back row, Becky McCormack, Patsy Morrison, Darlene Cook, Coach Gordon, Ruth Ann Ruble, and Delores Rucker. The spectators in the background are, left to right, Ezra Sea, J. R. Chesher, "Curly" Ruble, Dorothy Ruble, unidentified, and Jean Casey.

This Finchville team in the late 1940s included left to right; Charles Cheek, Charles McClain, Paul Donovan, William Stout, Harry Lefler, James Tingle, Michael Thompson, Thomas Huffman, William Floyd, Johnston Stout, and Coach James Burnett.

Finchville High School's basketball teams were cheered on by, clockwise from the top, June Krieger, Nellie McClain, Lillian Woods, and Nancy Durrett.

The Simpsonville High School team in 1941-42 included front row, left to right; Edington, Phillips, Herrick, Insko, Miller: back row, left to right; Carpenter, Casey, Mattox, Murray, Reid, and Coach Jimmy Burnett

Harold Tingle starred at Simpsonville High School in the mid-1950s, scoring 42 points in a game against Gallatin County.

This Cropper High School freshman team in the mid-1930s included front row, Bobby Moore, Bill Underwood, Morris Johnson, Suter Moore, and Carey Bellwood; back row, Dorsey Clark, John Davis, Paul Bottom, Ranny Baker, Leonard Lee, and Lester Bohannon.

This Bagdad High School team was the runner-up in the 1940 District Tournament. From left to right, front row, are "Pewee" Harper, Bobby Vanarsdale, Coach Jimmy Burnett, Eugene Lindsey, George N. Busey, and William Yount; back row, Manager Sam D. Weakley, Carlisle Barrickman, Earl Young Jr., Billy Vanarsdale, Jimmy McCarty, Bob Taylor, and Leland "Shag" Perkins.

Bagdad's Junior High School team included left to right, front row, Melvin Smither, Kenneth Ashby, "Peck" Poole, Jimmy Merchant and Bobby Ashby; back row, Billy Davis, Jack Vanarsdale, Melvin Harrod, and Coach Burnett.

Prior to the consolidation of the Shelby County schools, the only county high school which sent a team to the Kentucky High School State Basketball Tournament was Bagdad High School. The 1952 Bagdad Tigers won the 8th Regional Tournament by defeating LaGrange, 60-46, in the finals. Prior to that the Tigers slipped by Carrollton, 42-40, and Milton, 89-62. In the 30th District tournament, Bagdad defeated Waddy, 72-38, and edged Simpsonville, 59-56, in overtime. In the front row, left to right, are Manager Jimmy Hardin, Jimmy Wiley, Bronson Hardin, Marvin Brooks, Ed Thompson, Jimmy Moore, and Manager Roe Early; back row, Assistant Coach Arthur Moss, Principal William Detherage, Donald Wade, Clay Benton Young, Kenneth Slucher, Freddie Ruble, Robert Gray Early, and Coach Gayle Taft. The cheerleaders were Dorothy Perry, Mary Sue Shaw, Eloise Stivers, and Mary Jo Long.

These Bagdad High School cheerleaders were firing up the crowd in the 1960s.

The Lincoln Insitute team of 1959-60 counted on these players; from left to right, kneeling, are John O'Bannon and George Cottrell, trainers; standing, James Crayton, Clyde Mosbty, John Wakins, William Johnson, Daniel Thomas, William Spaulding, Coach Walter Gilliard, Wiliam Crayton, Jewell Logan, Carl Williams, Johnny Cunningham, Tyrone Handley, and Howard Barlow.

Lincoln Institute's football team of 1956-57 included first row, Stanley Williams, Charles Chatmond, Kenneth Hayden, Alfred Brooks, Charles Jones, Theodore Martin, Wallace Hill, Charles McAtee, Reginald Hicks, Cecil Davis, and John Lee; second row, George Bullitt, Oscar Patterson, Laphonso Williams, Henry Travis, George Cottrell, Charles Burkes, Ben Bridwell, Lura Roland, Robert Marshall, and Billy Slaughter; third row, James Perkins, trainer, Bobby Rickets, William Trowell, Duane Williford, Edward Chambers, Kenneth Andrews, Leon Smith, Ralph Willingham, Charles Benberry, Charles Walker, Earl Young, Louard Crumbaugh, Alex Chambers, Ray Barnette, and Herbert Garner, coach.

Varsity cheerleaders of 1956-57 at Lincoln Institute included clockwise, Laurice Smith, director, Sandra Wright, Carolyn Burkes, Carolyn Jackson, Barbara Stone, Anna Wooten, and Barbara Rudy.

For many years Lake Shelby, which was dedicated in 1949, was the principal water source for Shelbyville. That changed with the opening of Guist Creek Lake in the late 1950s. In 2008 the lake serves as a fishing, camping, and recreation facility.

The Shelbyville swimming pool opened for whites only in 1949. It was integrated in the early 1960s.

Elmo Head, standing on the left, helped operate the swimming pool in the early days. He served as baseball and golf coach, school principal and school board member, and was later President of the Farmers & Traders Bank.

The Mammoth Skating Rink was built in 1910 by George Saffell as the venue for many African-American events as well as a white prom, "Hop Club" dances and special events. Cab Calloway, Tina Turner, and The Drifters were among the nationally known artists who performed at the rink.

Susanne Van Stockum clears a jump in competition in Virginia around 1940. She was the wife of Brig. Gen. Ronald Van Stockum. She and the general and their two children took up residence at the ancestral home, Allen Dale farm, in 1970.

"Timely Tip," owned by Shelby County veterinarian Dr. A. L. Birch, finished 14th in the 1954 Kentucky Derby.

Shelby County's most famous horsewoman, Helen Crabtree, won several national titles in New York's Madison Square Gardens. She is shown here in 1980 on "Popular Time."

Shelbyville's state championship croquet team included, left to right, "Shorty" Howerton, Clayton Baker, French Smoot, Grover Skelton, and Estill Snyder.

The Shelbyville High School football team of 1930 lines up with; front row, "Zip" Craig, Capt. Bob Cowherd, Carroll Sanders, Fielding Ballard, Richard "Puss" Greenwell, Ben McMakin, and Jimmy Barnett; back row, Shelby Williams, Bruner Thompson, Garnett Radcliff, and H. A. "Gus" Barnett.

This Shelbyville High School team gave Coach C. Bruce Daniel his first CKC title in 1936. In the front, left to right, are; Vivian Harp, "Bud" Stratton, Kenneth Tipton, Hayden Igleheart, Herman Whitaker, Edwin Hall and Johnny Milton. The backfield includes Jerome Ritchie, Bill Shannon, Jesse Floyd, and Bill Gregg.

Legendary Shelbyville High School Coach Richard "Puss" Greenwell is flanked, left, by assistant coaches Allie Kays and Johnny Buckner, and, right, by two of his players, Morty Webb Jr. and Bob Montgomery. Greenwell coached teams that were undefeated in 1947, 1951, 1955, and 1957. CKC champions included the 1947, 1949, 1955, and 1962 teams.

Archie L. Ware, Jr., a licensed professional engineer by occupation, won Kentucky's Golden Gloves Championship in Lexington, Ky. in 1951.

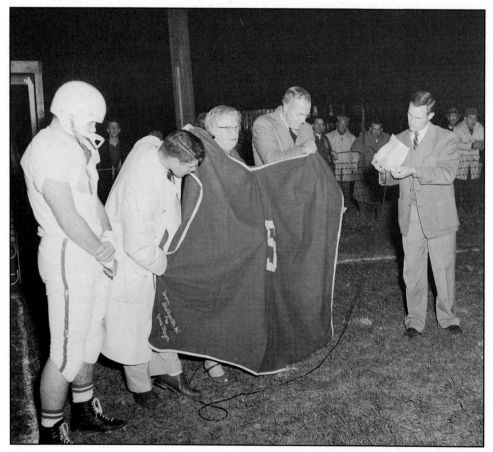

May and D. L. Green were recognized at halftime of a Shelbyville High School game by school alumni and friends. May and D. L. raised 10 children, with five playing at Shelbyville High School. Mrs. Green also served on the county and city school boards.

Willie Jenkins was a longtime friend and supporter of the Shelbyville High School football team.

The Shelbyville High School gym was opened in the early 1930s and was the scene of many triumphs (and a few defeats) for the local Red Devils. In 2006 it was renamed Evan Settle Memorial Gym after the veteran coach and teacher. Settle taught and coached from 1938 to 1942 and again from 1947 to 1972.

Charles Bradbury coached the Red Devils during the 1930s, and also owned Bradbury-Scofield Drug Store, and, later, Smith-McKenney Drug Co.

With Coach Evan Settle off to fight in World War II, Astor Tackett assumed the reigns of the 1942-43 Red Devils basketball team. The team won 20 and lost only nine. In the front row are, left to right, Allie Kays, Paul Briscoe, Bobby Green, Junie Sorrells, and Joe Shuck; second row, Assistant coach Bill Shannon, Lucien Palmer, Billy Pfost, Bill Johnston, Cal Schmidt, Ben Matthews, G. C. Brown, Manager Charles Henry Yount, and Coach Tackett. Top row, Dick Tygrett, Morgan Riggs, Ernest Searcy, and Bill Palmer.

Coach Evan Settle returned from the military in 1947 and guided the 1948 Red Devils to the school's first ever state tournament appearance. After beating Garrett in the opener, Shelbyville fell to Brewers High School, 58-37, in the quarterfinals. Brewers went on to win the state championship and, 60 years later, remained the only undefeated Kentucky boys high school basketball team. Pictured here, clockwise, beginning with the top photo, left side, are Johnny Buckner, Bob Logan, Mac Catlett, Martin Deim, Jimmy Mac Ratcliffe, Bill Green, Bo Moesser, James Martin, Billy Humston, and Bill Matthews.

Shelbyville's 1953 Kentucky State High School Basketball Tournament team included front, left to right, Achille Biagi, Joe Bowles, Charles "Skippy" Connell, George Catlett, Charles Mischler, "Pete" Raymond; standing, rear, Assistant Coach Al Jaggers, Bill Clemens, P. A. Wilson, Johnny Cowherd, Maurice Williard, Coach Evan Settle. In front is Manager Jimmy Chandler. This team defeated Owensboro in the tournament opener, and lost to Paducah Tilghman in the quarter-finals.

The 1956 Shelbyville Red Devils won the 8th Region title in 1956, and lost to Wayland and "King" Kelly in the opening round of the Kentucky State High School Basketball Tournament. Kelly scored 50 points, while Devils' ace Herbie Kays countered with 26. Coach Evan Settle frequently called Kays the most outstanding player who ever played for him. In the front row are; Kays, Bobby Swindler, "Shug" Hickman, Bill Clements, Donny Swigert; back row, Sammy West, Bobby Carter, Lewis Mathis Jr., Jess Frazier, Chester Ethington, Bill Frye, Bobby Joe Wright, Coach Settle.

For many years Jane Meyer entertained the coaches and players of all the Shelbyville High School teams at her Undulata home. From left to right in the early 1960s are school board member Bobby Stratton, Dennis Giles, Steve Pumphrey, head basketball coach Evan Settle, Rev. Fred Moffatt, and Superintendent Bill McKay.

Donnie Mason, Robert Jones, and Dean Chambers played in the Red Devils final game, in the 1975 Kentucky High School State Basketball Tournament.

Coach Evan Settle sent seven teams to the Kentucky High School State Basketball Tournament, including his final one in 1967. The Red Devils, who won 26 and lost only 4, included left to right, Randy Head, William Lewis, Howard Burley, Charles Marshall, Grant Hays, Assistant Coach Pumphrey; top row, left to right, Manager John Zachem, Herbert "Smitty" Johnson, James Ellis, Bob Montgomery, Bernard Brown, Charlie Matthews, manager John Scott Taylor, and cheerleader Susan Lea.

Jimmy Burnett, Guy Lea and Rodney "Doc" Whitaker get ready for an afternoon of tennis at the courts located adjacent to the former high school gym.

Jack and Ryland Byrd won the high school state tennis championship in 1941. Jack won the singles titles three straight years, 1939-1941. He was killed in a traffic accident near Versailles in the fall of 1948.

Coach Bruce Daniel provided guidance to these members of the Shelbyville High School tennis team: David Chadwell, Lindsey Logan, Jim Cleveland, Harriet Ballard, John Ellis, and Vance Burnett.

Norma Beasey was among the best local bowlers. Here she shows her form in 1976 at Shelby Lanes.

The 1973 Shelbyville High School girls tennis team included coach Betty Matthews, Lucy Greenwell, Piper Rogers, Debby Ellis, Nancy Easley, and Elberta Casey.

Four of the Shelbyville Country Club's top golfers for many years included left to right, Nathan Moberly, Howard Logan, Lucien Kinsolving, and Bob Logan. Kinsolving won the men's club championship 14 times, and Bob Logan twice. Howard Logan Jr. won the men's title four times and in 1976 won the Kentucky State High School Golf Championship.

Since the mid-1930s the lady golfers have been "teeing it up" each Tuesday morning during the summer months. In the 1960s this group included front row, Jean Logan, Bruce Logan, and Ethel Martin; back row, Hildreth Daniel, Helen Moberly, Sidney Combs, Susan Humston, Jean Cobb, Caroline Goodson, and Josephine Long. Bruce Logan won the Country Club's ladies championship 14 times, beginning in 1955 and ending in 1971. Jean Logan won the title five times and Helen Moberly won it twice.

This scorecard was used by the Shelbyville Golf and Fishing Club in the 1920s and early 30s which was located on the old Zaring farm on the Eminence Pike near "Cozy Corner."

The Shelbyville High School golf team in 1967 included left to right, Howard Hundley, Doug Potter, Alan Matthews, Charlie Matthews, Arthur Logan, Don Chatham, Dennis Long, Lee Kinsolving, Doug Logan, John Scott Taylor, Barney Hall, and Coach Steve Pumphrey.

The Shelbyville Country Club offered this view for golfers in the 1950s.

These young ladies were Shelbyville High School's last cheerleading team. At the top is Cheryl Greenwell, and below her Mary Stratton, the four girls are Sheree Martin, Lisa King, Kim McCarthy, and Karen Harrod. Gladys Ann Igleheart is on the floor.

Jane Meyer was a longtime sponsor, from 1948 to 1975, of the Shelbyville High School cheerleaders. Jane, who died in 1999, helped in the organization of the statewide cheerleading organization (KAPOS).

Shelbyville High School Cheerleaders were front, left to right; Nancy Shannon, Sheri Sandidge, Becky Frazier, Susan Lea, Meme Greenwell, Joy Stratton; standing, left to right; Brenda Pearce, Cheryl Clarke, Rose Guthrie, Lydia Hundley, Mary Beth Amyx, Linda Schmidt, Cecie Pearce, Betty Duncan, Connie Duncan, and Carol Crane.

Shelbyville cheerleaders included, first couple Debbie Cubert and Lyn Sandidge, second couple Lucy Buckner, Lydia Hundley, and third couple, Anita Payne, and Cheryl Clarke.

Ford Motor Co. Punt, Pass and Kick Winners saluted at the Pearce Motor Co. location on Main Street in the mid-1960s included left to right, Ronnie Bottom, Mark Ballard, Barney Hall, Larry Sorrels, Jimmy Keith Hanna, Bruce Moffatt, Graham Gee, Joe Bill Frazier, Johnny Booth, Burch Kinsolving, and Greg Hunter.

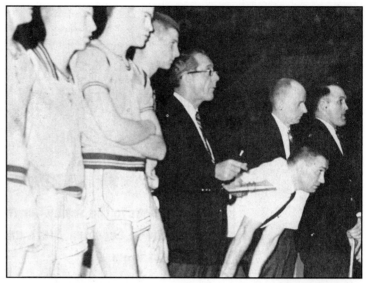

Bill Harrell coached the Shelby County Rockets during their most successful period in the school's basketball history. His inventiveness in setting up and calling plays by number from the bench started a trend among state coaches.

Coach Bill Harrell, in his shirt sleeves, had many an anxious moment during the Rockets 62-57 win over Louisville Male High for the state championship in 1966.

Cheerleaders and ballplayers celebrate the Rockets "day in the sun."

Coach Harrell and Jobie Miller display the championship trophy.

The 1966 basketball state champion Shelby County Rockets included front row, left to right, Bobby Burchfield, Johnny Edington, Gene Witt, Jobie Miller, Bill Busey, Terry Hall, Keith Stratton, manager; back row, Assistant Coach Arnold Thurman, Larry Glass, Hugh Smith, Jim Simons, Gene Edwards, Mike Casey, Mike Popp, Jamie Pickett, Ron Ritter, Bill Moffatt, Dave Bohannon, Assistant Coach Mitchell Bailey, head coach Bill Harrell.

The 1978 Shelby County Rockets, guided by Tom Creamer, defeated Covington Holmes in overtime to win the state high school basketball title. The team included, front row, left to right, kneeling, Arthur Sullivan, James Rockwell, Don Murphy, Mark Ashby, Gerry Davis, Kevin Armstrong; back row, Coach Creamer, Mike George, Norris Beckley, Austin Lee, Robert Davis, Charles Hurt, Pat Marshall, Maurice Way, Charlie Lecompte, Dale Kennedy. Coaches Marnel Moorman and Ron Kuhl are not pictured.

Charles Hurt was a standout basketball player at Shelby County High School. His turn-around shot at the buzzer enabled the Rockets to tie Covington Holmes in the 1978 finals of the Kentucky State High School Basketball Tournament. The team went on to win 68-66 in overtime. Hurt later starred at the University of Kentucky.

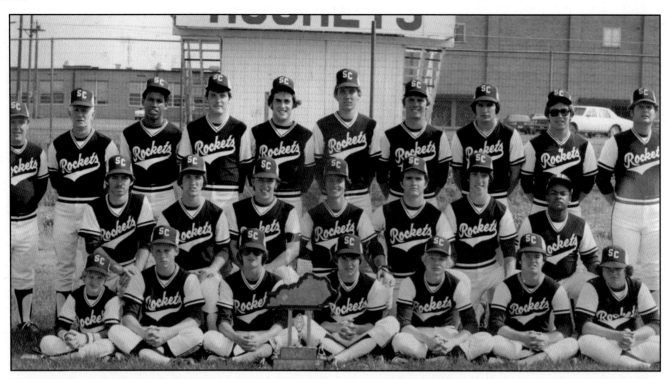

The 1979 State Champion Shelby County Rockets Baseball Team included front row, left to right, batboy Mike Rogers, Norman Munch, Kerry Whitehouse, Scott Clifford, Charles Clifton, Mark Chandler, Scott Corn, manager; middle row, Billy Reese, Keith Waford, David Bodine, Cody Tipton, Rusty Harrod, Greg Stratton, Lindsey Allen; back row, Assistant Coach Phil Bell, Assistant Coach Mitch Bailey, Mike Marshall, Perry Joe Nutt, Greg Jennings, James Ray Wiley, Joe Long, Tracy Driver, Brian Mitchell, Head Coach Hubert Pollett. The Rockets won 18 and lost only 2. The team won the regional tournament by defeating Frankfort, 8-4, the semi-state by rolling over Connor, 5-0, and the state title by edging Murray, 7-5, on Tracy Driver's home run. Driver was voted the tournament's Most Valuable Player.

The 1987 Shelby County High School 4A State Football Champions, coached by Tom Becherer, included in uniform, left to right, front row, Donnie Mason, Chris Waldridge, Ron Simmons, Chad Schott, Herb Fletcher, Mike Stoner, Ray Marshall, Reggie Hicks, Chris Waford, Steve Hall, Matt Crockett, Monty Wood, Darryle Hicks, Nelson Robinson, Steve Russell; second row, Jeff Hayden, Tom Bailey, Mark Wilson, Shawn Riley, Melvin Hall, Monty Walker, Mickey Perry, Matt Kehrt, Tony Griffin, Ralph Stone, Gary Harrison, Geoffrey Manica, Greg Young, Keith Owens, Edmund Becherer; third row, Darrell Perry, Don Marshall, Jeff Conan, Eric Sutherland, Chris Cottongim, Brian Stivers, Chad Adams, Marcus Stoner, Tommy Thompson, Charles Warfield, Lee Hankins, Dan Druin, Chris Chanda, Mack Rayburn, Mike Rogers, Brent Wilson, Scott Lawson, Brian King. The assistant coaches were Hubert Pollett, Phil Bell, Mike Breidet, and Boyd Phillips.

Tradition in Shelbyville since 1942

W. CROMWELL'S
MENS CLOTHING

525 WASHINGTON ST.
633-4440
EST. 1983

THE COUNTRY LADY
WOMENS CLOTHING

525 WASHINGTON ST.
633-5239
EST. 1978

W.J. ANDRIOT'S
PAINT WALLPAPER BLINDS

718 MAIN
633-1944
EST. 2005

ANDRIOT'S COACH HOUSE
EST. 1978

BIAGI'S

Thirteen years old, alone, and knowing no English, Annibale Biagi emigrated in 1909 from Lucca, Italy to the Untied States. He made his way to Shelbyville where he first found work serving ice cream in a local restaurant. He subsequently operated a wholesale produce business, supplying local restaurants with fruits and vegetables.

In 1927 he founded The Biagi Company to sell tires and batteries. The store was originally located at the corner of 6th & Washington Streets, when 6th Street was a major hub for the town's commercial activity. During the remainder of the 20th century the company would grow under the care of three generations, and eventually evolve into one of the area's largest appliance and electronics dealers. After a few years the company also went into the bedding and mattress business. .

The Biagi Company's initial venture into appliances occurred in 1937 when the firm began marketing Maytag wringer washers. In fact, the store still has on hand the original franchise agreement signed by Eli Maytag.

These gasoline-powered washers were sold on consignment from Maytag, which received the profits from the sale. Biagi's profited only from selling the oil that was needed to operate the washer's gasoline engine.

During the 1940s the transition into an appliance and electronics store continued. By then the company had added Frigidaire appliances and RCA radios. In 1948 the company sold the first television set in Shelby County. A crowd gathered at Biagi's on Thanksgiving Day 1948 to watch the area's first live television transmission – a broadcast of the Male-Manual High Schools' football game By WAVE-TV in Louisville.

That original 1948 RCA television, with an 8-inch picture tube, is on display at the store.

In 1944 The Biagi Company moved from its original location to its current location at 541 Main Street. The company was growing and needed more room to display its expanding selection of merchandise. In 1954 the building underwent a major renovation. At that time the storefront was completely redesigned, and the interior was remodeled, which included opening it up to access to the second floor from within the building. Over the years, as the business continued to grow, adjoining properties on Main, 6th, and Washington Streets were purchased to provide more sales, service and parking areas.

During the 1950s, under the direction of Annibale and Alberta's oldest son, Vincent, the transformation into a full-fledged appliance and electronics store was completed. By then tires and batteries had become a sideline.

Vincent, who had been involved with the home appliance industry since its infancy, would continue to guide the business for over 40 years. During that same time, his brother Hugh was responsible for the company's service department. The two brothers witnessed many firsts in the appliance and electronics industry. Items that are now taken for granted were introduced to area households. Refrigerators replaced iceboxes, automatic washers replaced washtubs, and electric ranges replaced wood-burning stoves. They likewise introduced conveniences such as microwave ovens, room air conditioners, color television, video recorders, and satellite television.

A third generation of Biagi's, Vincent's sons Stephen and Robert, continue the family's tradition of providing quality products and service.

Stephen is a 1973 graduate of Notre Dame University, and Robert a 1978 graduate of the United of Kentucky. Each started working in the store as a teenager.

Biagi's belongs to a National Buying Group of 7,000 dealers across the country. Belonging to this group enables Biagi's to compete with anyone and everyone on price. But when it comes to service, Biagi's proudly believes that it stands above the rest.

Stephen and Robert continue a proud tradition of Biagi quality products and service.

In 1944 Biagi's moved to its present location at 541 Main Street.

1906: Coldwell Banker Real Estate was founded in San Francisco, California.

1923: Italian Renaissance home at 820 Main Street, Shelbyville, Kentucky, was constructed and became home to the McCormack, Hayes and Walls families until 1986.

1986: 820 Main Street was home to Swan House Antiques providing home décor items

1995: 820 Main Street became the home of the Coldwell Banker Larry K Rogers family of Realtors

2008: We invite you to come and tour our home at 820 Main Street. One of our friendly and professional Realtors will be happy to help you with your family's home needs.

COLDWELL BANKER - CELEBRATING OVER 100 YEARS OF SUCCESS

820 MAIN STREET - PROVIDING FAMILY HOME NEEDS FOR 85 YEARS

LARRY K. ROGERS REALTY INC

SIMPSONVILLE OFFICE
502-722-1696

SHELBYVILLE OFFICE
502-633-4696

Crabtree Farm

Established 1957
Simpsonville, Kentucky

Charles, Helen and Redd Crabtree

**Redd, Anne, Nancy, Susan Crabtree Fenton
and Casey Crabtree**

*Proudly serving the American Saddlebred Industry
from Shelby County Kentucky
"The American Saddlebred Capital of the World"
for over 50 years*

8690 Shelbyville Road · P.O Box 440 · Simpsonville, Kentucky · 40067

Welcome to Crestview

Since 1965, our facility has assured residents are provided with the highest quality care.

Our home–like facility is staffed with caring professionals who can provide both short and long-term care. We have excellent therapy and restorative programs, which have allowed us to discharge many residents back into the community.

The uniqueness of providing health care in a small facility enables our staff to meet the individual needs of each resident. At Crestview, each resident is treated with the dignity and compassion they deserve.

Crestview has received numerous awards through the years, including Kentucky Statewide Facility of the Year.

Contact Crestview at (502) 633-2454 to arrange a personal tour at your convenience.

 **CRESTVIEW**
Rehabilitation & Nursing Center

1871 Midland Trail • Shelbyville
(502) 633-2454

The things we do for *improving with age.*

WORKING HARD FOR 150 YEARS

Whether it's next week, next month or next decade, you have plans for your life. As you work toward that future, you can have confidence knowing Fifth Third Bank has a history of turning dreams into realities. 150 years to be exact. That's important, because you should feel as certain about your bank's resources and determination as you feel about your own. The way you can feel about us. Give us a call at 502-633-4652 or visit 53.com to see what we can do for you.

FIFTH THIRD BANK

The things we do for dreams.™

53.com

232

Proud to be part of the Shelby County
& Simpsonville Community

Golden Creek Farms

PO Box 100 • Simpsonville KY 40067

For Over 100 Years, Joining Together for a Happier, Healthier Community

For more than three generations, Jewish Hospital Shelbyville has been providing excellent health care options. Thanks to the people of Shelby, Spencer and Henry Counties, Jewish Hospital Shelbyville is this area's health care provider of choice.

Providing:

- 24-Hour, 7 Days a Week Emergency Services
- Critical Care
- State of the art MRI, CT, Ultrasound, Digital Mammography & Bone Density
- Fully-Equipped Cardiac & Pulmonary Rehabilitation
- State of the art Stress Test/Nuclear Cardiology
- Sleep Medicine
- Advanced Surgeries, including Laser, Endoscopy & Laparoscopy
- Comprehensive Gynecology
- Clinical Laboratory
- Skilled Nursing Facility
- Frazier Rehab Institute (Physical, Occupational & Speech Therapies)
- EmployCare™ Occupational Medicine
- Wound Healing Center

 Jewish Hospital Shelbyville

727 Hospital Drive
Shelbyville, Kentucky 40065
(502) 647-4000

www.jhsmh.org

Proud to be a Part of Shelby County History Since 1925

Logan's is a family owned and operated business that was started in Shelbyville in 1925 by William Lindsey Logan Sr. Over the years the company has remained in the family and is currently operated by his grandsons, Arthur Logan and Howard Logan, Jr.

The company began as a one plant operation that served the laundry and dry cleaning needs of families with home deliveries. Logan's currently has two facilities operating in Shelby County. Logan's Uniform, Inc. rents and processes garments, area protection and logo mats, dust mops and shop towels for a variety of businesses and industries and employs approximately 60 people.

Logan's Healthcare, Inc. rents and processes linen to hospitals, nursing homes, clinics and healthcare related businesses and employs approximately 140 people. The two plants are located on Harry Long Road in the Pearce Industrial Park.

Bill Logan, Jr., Arthur Logan, Howard Logan Sr., Howard Logan Jr., Bob Logan. Photo taken in May 2005, courtesy of Sentinel-News.

Logan's
UNIFORM RENTAL
1210 Harry Long Drive
Shelbyville, KY 40065

Logan's Uniform Rental
1210 Harry Long Road
Shelbyville, Kentucky 40065
(502) 633-3616

Logan's Healthcare
1240 Harry Long Road
Shelbyville, Kentucky 40065
(502) 633-0298

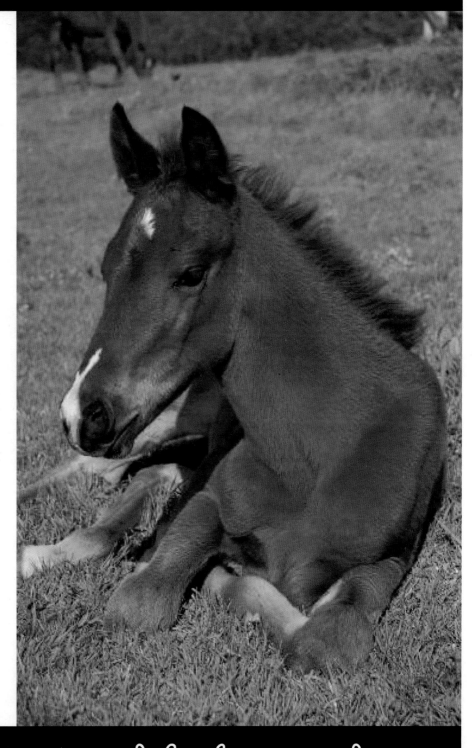

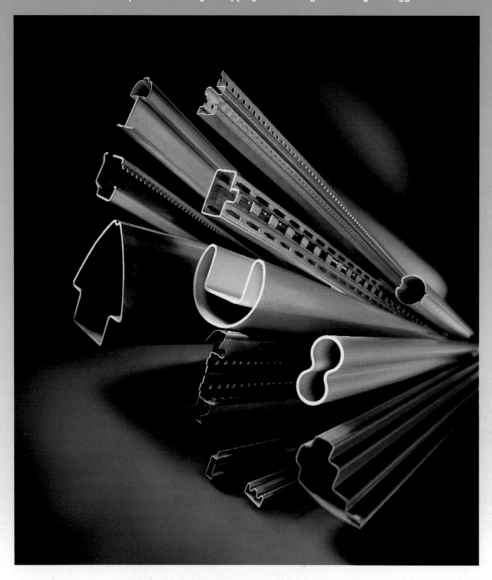

238

Wakefield Scearce Galleries

Science Hill

Julia Ann (Hieronymus) Tevis, a brilliant young educator, founded Science Hill School in 1825. She had married John Tevis, a young Methodist minister in their home state of Virginia. After their marriage, John was called to pastor at Louisville's Methodist church at the Falls of the Ohio.

While traversing the trail from Virginia to Louisville, the young couple discovered Shelbyville as so many had before them. In Shelbyville, Julia vowed to continue her teaching career by tutoring young girls who made their homes in the Kentucky wilderness. But she planned to teach her charges more than the traditional "gentle lady's education" of reading, writing and the social graces; she also endeavored to teach her students the sciences, something unheard of in those times. Legend portrays Julia on a hill to the rear of her cousin Lloyd's property betstowing a name to her new home: Science Hill School.

On March 25, 1825, Julia opened her school with great anxiety about the size of her first class. To her surprise, 20 girls enrolled on the first day. With the school's immediate success, John requested to be transferred from his larger Louisville pastorate to the smaller Methodist Chapel in Shelbyville, only a few yards from Julia's school.

John began to assist his wife in the management of her growing school and eventually facilitated an extensive expansion between 1826 and 1846. Today, Science Hill remains little changed.

In 1879, Dr. Wiley Taul Poynter undertook the operation of Science Hill School. The new administrator improved the leadership curriculum until Science Hill became one of the pre-eminent girls' preparatory institutions in America.

The building was once again expanded and was even included on the famous Lyceum Lecture Circuit from 1888 until around 1938. This prestigious accolade brought hundreds of the most famous and distinguished speakers,

writers, and educators of the time to the school's Chapel. With five other private schools and the Lyceum Circuit, Shelbyville became quite a cultural center, even featuring an Opera House at 7th and Main Streets.

Unfortunately, the hardships of the Great Depression doomed many schools across the United States to failure. After 114 of continuous operation, Science Hill graduated its last class in 1939. During its time Science Hill School had established a reputation of greatness for its contribution to education and culture. The lives of those girls who graduated from the prestigious school have affected the development of every state in the Union.

After the school's 1939 closing, most of the premises became a residential inn. Misses Juliet and Harriet Poynter, daughters of Dr. Wiley Poynter, retained only the most western portion, the original structure, as their home. They were born in Shelbyville in the late 1800s, and they would die nearly 100 years later.

The History of Wakefield-Scearce

In 1947 Mark Wakefield and Mark Scearce leased the extreme eastern portion of Science Hill known as the Chapel or Lecture Hall from the Misses Poynter. Together they founded Wakefield-Scearce Galleries with the intent of selling antiques of British origin. After four years, Mr. Wakefield retired from the business he helped found, but his name and his inspiration remain with the Galleries.

Mark J. Scearce continued to operate the retail antique business and was able to purchase the eastern portion of the property in 1961. Four years later he purchased the remainder of the property on the condition that the Misses Poynter be allowed to reside in the west wing until their deaths.

The property had fallen into disrepair since the school's closing in 1939. Indeed, the building had not even been painted in nearly 40 years,

and the plumbing and wiring, originally installed in the early 1900s, were dangerously antiquated.

Thus, upon the purchase of the property, Mr. Scearce launched an 18 months restoration in which nearly 75 miles of new wiring was laid, 14 miles of new copper plumbing installed, and 700 gallons of paint used in the single coating of the building.

Between 1981 and 1982 Mr. Scearce launched a new 15 month restoration of the West Wing following the death of Miss Harriet Poynter in 1982 at the age of 99 (Miss Juliet had died in 1974 at the age of 93.). Upon the renovation completion in the autumn of 1983, four new shops were opened to the public in what is now called the Poynter Wing.

The Courtyard

Today Science Hill is divided into three major sections: the Gallery, the Courtyard, and the Dining Room. The Gallery still serves in its original retail capacity: selling primarily British antiques to the American public. The Courtyard is home to five shops that sell fashionable apparel, silver, linens, and even Christmas ornaments. The Dining Room makes use of the original kitchen and dining hall to serve dinner to any guest of this historic place.

Historic Science Hill now houses one of the largest collections of English antique furniture, silver, and accessories in the United States. Its dining room is always full of good food and its shops are staffed by wonderful people. Today's genteel use of the Science Hill property is a fitting monument to a place so rich with history, housing auspicious institutions of education, culture, and gracious living for nearly 200 years.

240

Shelby County Fiscal Court

S ince their first meeting on October 15, 1792, the judges and magistrates who comprise Shelby County's Fiscal Court have played an exceedingly important role in shaping this county's wonderful and enduring history.

It has been their responsibility to make sure Shelby Countians enjoy good roads, pay their fair share of taxes, and live in a county where excellent planning and zoning have made it a great place to live, go to school, earn a living, raise a family, worship freely and enjoy many recreational opportunities.

The Fiscal Court has also played a leadership role in bringing many industries to Shelby County, and these industries, in turn, have provided the kinds of worthwhile jobs that have made it possible for our high school graduates who choose to go on to college to find local employment when they graduate.

County Judge/Executive Robert Rothenburger, the Shelby County Fiscal Court, and all of those who have been elected to or are employed by county government take pride in our local history and appreciate this opportunity to salute those who have photographed the past as guardians of our heritage. They have left a wonderful legacy for us to treasure in the many years to come.

2007:
Bought 110 acres on US 60 West as campus for three future school buildings

2005:
Built Clear Creek Elementary off Old Mount Eden Road
Renovation to Wright Elementary
Addition/renovation to Simpsonville Elementary

2008:
6200 students, 900 employees, one high school, one alternative school, two middle schools, six elementary schools, three preschool sites
Design/development phase under way for new secondary center on new campus
Construction under way for new campus boulevard

2004:
Closed Southside Elementary (circa 1957 – reopened in 2006 due to increased enrollment)
Restored Shelbyville High School as Central Administrative Office

2003:
Built Athletic Complex on Burks Branch Road

2001:
Renovation/addition to Area Technology Center (circa 1968)

1991:
Converted Cropper into alternative/ day treatment school
Developed Preschool program with education reform

2002:
Closed Northside Elementary (circa 1939)
Built Painted Stone Elementary off LaGrange Road

2000:
Built new West Middle off LaGrange Road

1992:
Major renovation and addition to Shelby County High School

1989:
Consolidated Bagdad, Cropper and Henry Clay elementary schools and built Heritage Elementary near Peytona

1918:
Built Shelbyville High School on West Main Street (additions in 1952 and 1964)

1988:
Built new Simpsonville Elementary on Shelbyville Road

1960:
Consolidation of county high schools to open Shelby County High School on US 60 East

1980:
Built Wright Elementary on Rocket Lane

1967:
Lincoln Institute closed (circa 1912) in Simpsonville with African-American students transferring to city and county school systems

1975:
Merged city and county school systems: turned Shelbyville High into West Middle and Upper Elementary into East Middle (both grades 6-8)

SHELBY COUNTY PUBLIC SCHOOLS
Educational excellence in the future will stem from solid foundations of the past and present

James Neihof, Superintendent ~ 1155 West Main Street, Shelbyville KY 40065 ~ 502-633-2375 ~ www.shelby.kyschools.us

S helby County's largest CPA firm traces its beginning back to 1954 when Andrew Johns, a certified public accountant, founded the company in an office on the second floor of the old Armstrong Agency building on Main Street. Later, he moved his offices to Science Hill on Washington Street.

Johns was joined by Joe Sutherland in 1963 and later Sutherland passed the examination which led to his certification as a CPA. The two men formed a partnership, Johns and Sutherland, in July 1967, and for the next few years the firm was a statewide leader in adopting new technology for the preparation of tax returns.

It was in 1980 that Johns and Sutherland became the first CPA firm in Kentucky to prepare computerized in-house tax returns.

A graduate of Bagdad High School (1957) and the University of Kentucky (1963) with a degree in Business Administration, Mr. Sutherland became the sole owner of the business when Mr. Johns retired in 1982. Previously, in 1977, they had erected a contemporary building for their practice at 1020 Washington Street.

Today, the firm employs three CPAs in addition to Sutherland. They are Reba Kelley, Ron Yount, and Kyle Roberts.

J. Sutherland, PSC • 1020 Washington Street • Shelbyville, Kentucky
(502) 633-3967
"The Solution to Your Business and Tax Problems"

243

TRACY'S HOME FURNISHINGS
Fine Furniture, Accessories, Bedding & Appliances for the Home

days repairing radios, televisions and appliances. Neighbors learned of his skills, and began bringing him all manner of household gadgets to repair. He truly enjoyed this work and, in 1950, decided to open a service business.

He had his first repair shop near the corner of Tenth and Henry Clay Streets, keeping it open part time. Margaret served as his bookkeeper. When J.B. retired from Greyhound after 17 years, he moved his shop to 416 Main Street. He and Margaret sold televisions and appliances and later added furniture and mattresses to their inventory. They briefly moved to the basement of Lawson's Department Store, before purchasing the Ratcliffe's Furniture building at 604 Main Street, where Tracy's is still located. Coincidentally, this building was once part of the Armstrong Hotel, where General Henry Denhardt was gunned down by the Garr brothers in 1937. J.B.'s father, Jeptah Tracy, was the arresting officer in that case, and his younger brother, Bruce Tracy, was an eyewitness to the shooting. Business thrived in their new location and the Tracy's youngest son, Mike, came to work with them full time after attending Eastern Kentucky University and receiving a degree in electronics from United Electronics Institute.

In November 1973, the Tracy's building was gutted by fire. No one was injured, but all inventory and bookkeeping records were lost. Though devastated, J.B. and Margaret began the hard work of rebuild-

ing their business. Thanks to the support of loyal customers, Tracy's emerged from tragedy to grow stronger. A few years later they were able to purchase the adjoining building at 606 Main Street, which had been Newberry's Dime Store. This building continues to serve as Tracy's main furniture showroom.

J.B. Tracy passed away in 1988. His wife continued running their business well into her eighties. Mike began taking over more and more management duties, and in 2000 Mrs. Tracy turned the store completely over to their son. Mike Tracy continues to lead his family's business today. Like his father, Mike provides service for everything he sells. When not doing service work, he interacts with customers in his store, maintaining its friendly atmosphere. While still known for appliances and electronics, Tracy's has greatly expanded their furniture and bedding categories. They are also becoming known for their wide array of unique home accessories. The store underwent interior and exterior renovations during 2004 and 2005.

While adapting to economic fluctuations and changing consumer demands, J.B. and Margaret Tracy were successful because they gave excellent service and treated all customers with respect. With business still going strong after 58 years, Tracy's Home Furnishings will continue to adapt to the ever-changing retail market, but will always be guided by J.B. and Margaret Tracy's philosophy of serving with integrity.

The Main Street store now known as Tracy's Home Furnishings originally started as a repair shop on Tenth Street. It was a hobby that eventually became a second career for founder J.B. Tracy.

A native of Shelbyville, J.B. was forced to leave school after the eighth grade to help support his family during the Depression. He deeply regretted this, but remained an avid reader throughout his life. He met Margaret Hall, from Cropper, at the Shelby County Fair. "He asked me to ride the Ferris wheel," Margaret says. "We started seeing each other and we never stopped." After they were married, J.B. and Margaret lived in Louisville. He worked as a driver for Greyhound, studying radio and electronics in his spare time. After moving back to Shelbyville, J.B. spent his off

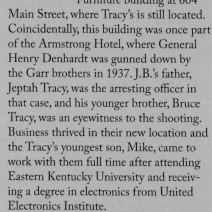

Undulata Farm
Zaring Mill Road

An American Saddlebred Horse Farm
founded by the Weissinger family in 1895.
Proud to be a part of Shelby County,
The American Saddlebred
Capital of the World

~Edward R. (Hoppy) Bennett~

The Upper Room Bible Class

In 1925 Robert F. Matthews and six men – W. P. Anderson, Albert Ramsey, John Grubbs, Ellis McGinnis, Bernard Tackett and Robert Yount -- gathered in the kitchen of the old First Christian Church sanctuary to begin what would prove to be an extraordinary Sunday school class.

The idea for an Upper Room Class grew out of the heart and mind of Mr. Matthews who, while attending the University of Michigan from 1915 until his graduation from law school six years later, attended a class of the same name. taught by "Father Iden" in his home in Ann Arbor. It was in this class that Mr. Matthews developed a love and a curiosity about the Holy Bible.

From this simplest of beginnings and this handful of men, The Upper Room began to grow. The class welcomed men from all creeds and denominations who had a natural desire to learn of God.

And so it was that, only 22 years later, on a Sunday morning in November 1947, 123 men assembled to learn more of the Bible and to enjoy the fellowship of a group of men who, for some, represented the most important substance in their lives.

Beginning in 1926, the Upper Room conducted what, for a long time, was the only Easter Sunrise Service in Shelby County. By 1941, with the nation troubled by the specter of global wars, the service had become the largest single religious experience in Shelbyville. The sanctuary of the First Christian Church was filled and extra chairs were put in the aisles for the worshippers from city and county churches.

Many of those who appeared on the platform at Easter Sunrise had never before appeared before such a large audience. And it was class tradition that each speaker had to give his part of the program – the Invocation, the Story of the Resurrection, the Easter Prayer, and the Benediction -- from memory, a fact which made for many a nervous moment.

From 1926 through 1957 Mr. Matthews gave the primary message. Beginning in 1958 class members and then ministers from the various churches in the city began giving the inspiration talk.

Music was always an important part of the Eastern Sunrise Service. Among the many soloists who are remembered fondly are Lewis Mathis Jr., Harvey Sutherland, and Zerelda Matthews. Favorite selections included "The Holy City," "My God and I", and "Were You There."

The Chapel was dedicated to the memory of three class members - Bailey Cowherd, Robert Newton and "Monk" Maddox - who died in combat during World War II. The dream of worshiping in their own chapel was fulfilled in 1948 with the dedication of The Upper Room Memorial Chapel, as part of the new education building. Money for the chapel's construction had come in from all points of the globe during World War II. The first organ for the Chapel was installed in 1950. The chapel also stemmed from the inspiration of Rev. Wayne Bell, the church minister at the time, and a regular visitor to the class.

Mr. Matthews once described the men of the Upper Room Class as a "congenial group of carpenters, farmers, painters, bankers, lawyers, doctors, college students, mail carriers, accountants, executives and mechanics." He said that as a whole, they lack piety, have a faith their lips seldom profess, and the natural desire to learn of God in this world and the next. They are seekers of the Truth."

Each Easter service beginning in 1940, the class sang "In the Sweet Bye and Bye," in memory and honor of those who had died. On Easter morning 2007 when the class met for the final time, with only four members present, "In the Sweet Bye and Bye" was sung one last time, honoring more than 100 members of the Upper Room Bible Class who had crossed to the other shore.

Below: In this 1946 photo are left to right class founder Robert F. Matthews, First Christian Church Minister Rev. Wayne Bell, and long-time class President and charter member Robert Yount.

ACKNOWLEDGEMENTS

We are grateful to the following individuals, businesses, institutions, and countless others for your support in publishing *Portrait of the Past – A Pictoral History of Shelby County, Kentucky 1865-1980*.

Kathy Adams
Pauline Adams
William Allen
Ruth Porter Allender
Amy Alvarez
Bill Andriot
Bob Andriot
Mary Atwood
Helen Ballard
Betsy Lou Baxter
Daisy Baxter
Wayne Bell
George Best
Steve Biagi
Dudley Bottom, Jr.
Betty Bowles
Buddy Bowles
Ruth Briscoe
G. C. Brown
Donna Bruner
Doris Burk
Vance Burnett
Harriet Ballard Butterbaugh
Faye Callahan
Tony Carriss
Betty Carter
Judy Casey
Betty Jean Chatham
Henry Cleveland
Katherine Cleveland
Mrs. Roy Collings, Jr.
Betsy Lou Baxter Collins
Steve Collins
Mrs. Lewis Cottingim
Crabtree Farm
Linzie Craig
Susan Hayes Crecelius
Deanie Crouch
Don Cubert
Roland Dale
Rosella Yeager
　　Cunningham Davis
Sally Davis
Jamie Donaldson

Rosa Douglas
Mrs. J. C. Dugan
Bill Ellis
Steve Ellis
Terry Ethington
Sarahbeth Farabee
Lou B. Finnell
Nancy Finney
Debbie Fitzgerald
Willie Fleming
Mrs. Jack Frazier
Ann Gibbs
Ann Graham
John Graham
Whitie Gray
Bonnie Gray
Loula Guthrie
Neil Hackworth
Sharon Hackworth
Neal Hammon
Curtis Hardesty
Edward Hayes
Shirley Hayes
Ermine Herrick
Ann Miller Hildreth
Nancy Hill
Lamar Hundley
Libby Igleheart
Ted Igleheart
Sherry Jelsma
Waddy Jesse
Burch Kinsolving
Doris Kinsolving
Margaret Kirk
Dr. James Klotter
Mrs. Howard Lawson
Jack Lawson
Eve Lawson-Lewis
Ann Logan
William Lindsey Logan
Charles Long
Lucy Long
Sue Long
David Mathis

Lewis Mathis
Ben G. Matthews
Betty Matthews
Charlie Matthews
Lisa Matthews
Mary Lou Mattingly
Ellis McGinnis
Michael McGinnis
Catherine McKinley
Hart Megibben
Alwyn Miller
Peggy Miller
Mary E. Mitchell
Kathy Moore
Rhelda Moore
Mrs. Marnel Moorman
Louise Slucher Morris
James Mulcahy
Edmund Myles
John David Myles
Mary David Myles
B. J. Nethery
Rusty Newton
Vivian Overall
Ann Patterson
Robert Pearce
Mae Peniston
Hubert Pollett
Libby Pollett
Duanne Puckett
Charles Randolph
Augusta Rhodes
Bill Rogers Studio
Alfred S. Joseph Rothchild III
The Rothchild Family
Dorothe Gruber Roulston
Gary Ruble
Tony Ruble
Judy Scearce
Mark Scearce
Calvin Schmidt
William L. Shannon
Arletta Shouse
Grover Skelton

R. L. Spencer
Nell Smith
Mansfield Stoghill
Gary Steinhilber
Bill Stout
Judy Price Stout
Helen Stratton
Mike Tracy
Lydia Hundley Turner
Ben Allen Thomas
Emily Thomas
Katherine Tingle
Brig. Gen. Ronald R. Van
　　Stockum
Leona Waits
Bob Walters
Jean Ware
Eleanor Warford
John Wesley Williams
Otho Williams
Wolf, Gretter, Cusick Hill
　　Studio
Ghost Railroads of Kentucky
The Filson Club
*The Louisville Courier-
　　Journal and Times*
*The New History of Shelby
　　County, Kentucky*
Shelby County Schools
Shelby County Life
Shelby County Government
Shelbyville City
　　Government
The Kentucky Historical
　　Society
The Shelby County
　　Historical Society
The Shelby County Public
　　Library Photographic
　　Archives
The Shelby News
The Shelby Record
The Shelby Sentinel
The Sentinel-News

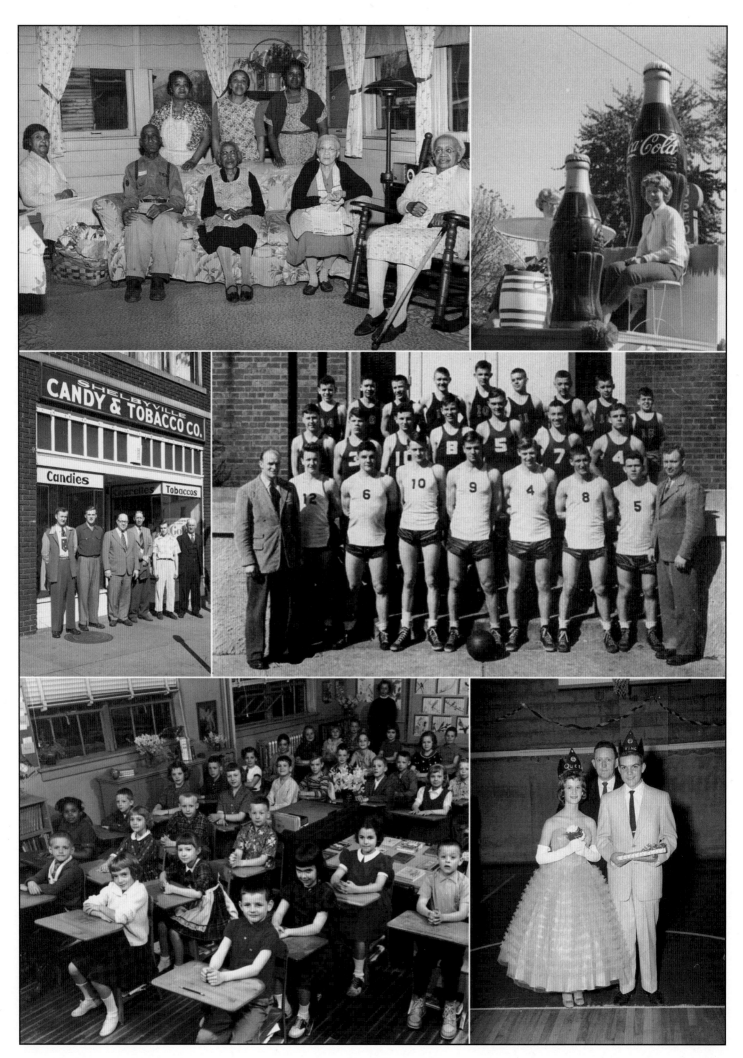

249

INDEX

250